Last updated on March 3, 2011.

ISBN 1-60658-015-9
ISBN 978-1-60658-015-8

Printed by:
KOINONIA ASSOCIATES
7809 Timber Glow Trail
Knoxville, TN 37938

RAISED INTO NEW LIFE, PART 1

YOU CAN BE RAISED INTO NEW LIFE WITH CHRIST

The index information is at the end of the book rather than here, in order that the text itself will be first available.

FOREWORD

A favorite Bible verse for most who know Jesus is John 3:16. It reads, "For God so loved the world, that he gave his only Son, that whoever believes in HIM should not perish but have eternal life" John 3:16—(ESV). Some who read the verse emphasize the word "believes." The correct emphasis is on "HIM," Jesus, God's unique Son. This book aims to help readers see that emphasis. It is good for us to realize that humans are not perfect. We CAN be wrong. We CAN misunderstand what we hear or read. On the other hand, we can learn truth and walk in truth. Some things are wrong. Some people are wicked.

Those who now know there is a God, a God who hates and punishes wrong-doing, may "put sin to death" by turning away from sin and seeking a new birth as a Christ-follower. Jesus tells of the need (John 3:3-8). Every sinner needs a new birth of water and spirit. Here we discuss new birth and the life which follows. A first step toward eternal life in Christ is to realize that God is good. Jesus came to earth to help people know that God is love. He punishes sin. He rewards those who choose the "good" life. God is good. People also can be good. We choose. Either good or bad. Selfish or unselfish. Usually most of us are both good and bad.

It's SINNERS who are offered new life by Jesus. We speak here about the new life He offers. Repentance is essential to changed life! Both Peter (Acts 2:38) and Paul (1 Corinthians 12:12,13) point out that God's "gift" of eternal life in Jesus is given to us following our new birth of water and spirit. The new birth of spirit is called repentance. This is more than just a change of mind! Repentance is a change of the will. It's a change of intention and direction. No longer selfish. Now selfless. Death to sin must *precede* the NEW life in Christ. Love of self must go.

Who knows better than Jesus does what is required to enter His kingdom? We do well to learn from HIM. Salvation comes to those who believe in Jesus, that He lived as a man on earth after having been the actual and active creator of the earth, that He was put to death and then He Himself was raised up into NEW LIFE. Realizing our sin, we're saved by faith in Jesus when we turn away from sin and choose new birth to make HIM our Lord for life. Then we can enjoy life *with Jesus!* We serve Him and enjoy it because we love Him. The NEW LIFE is lived in love. Jesus loves us. Jesus wants us to love one another. He wants us to love even the unlovely and the unloving, just as He does. Here we point to simple scriptural truths concerning entering life with Jesus.

In Bible quotations in this study, "Spirit" is sometimes changed by this author to "spirit." The original Greek does not capitalize the word. Translators do capitalize when they think the meaning is God's Spirit. When I see the translators are wrong, I choose to remove their capitalization.

I explain my thinking about this in the study in this book, "Were You *Elected* to Salvation?" God invites ALL to come and be saved! He doesn't "give" faith to some and not to others. He freely offers GRACE to all. Every person is welcome to hear, believe, and obey the gospel of Christ and be saved! This study invites you to think more about the life which comes by dying to sin and being *RAISED* INTO NEW LIFE.

PREFACE

JESUS SAYS He will become a guest in our life IF we experience a "new birth" of water and spirit. ... He said, "Truly, truly, I say to you, unless one is born again he cannot see the kingdom of God." Nicodemus said to him, "How can a man be born when he is old? Can he enter a second time into his mother's womb and be born?" Jesus answered, "Truly, truly, I say to you, *unless one is born of water and spirit, he cannot enter the kingdom of God.* That which is born of flesh is flesh, and that which is born of spirit is spirit. Do not marvel that I said to you, 'You must be born again.' The wind blows where it wishes, and you hear its sound, but you do not know where it comes from or where it goes. So it is with everyone who is born of spirit." John 3:3-8—(ESV) as edited.

Jesus offers to live within us after a new birth of water and spirit. In this book we tell about the NEW BIRTH and its results. All Christians became so by being born again. Surely we will recognize CHANGE in our thinking, our speaking, and our actions when we realize that Jesus now walks within us! Existence dramatically changes when a baby is born. Light is seen. Breathing begins! Hunger awakens. Newborn Christians are "babes in Christ."

We first examine briefly Bible examples of conversion to Christ, then move on to learning from apostles of Christ more about being RAISED INTO NEW LIFE. Are not all of us sinners? Only what Jesus did on the cross makes our salvation possible. Men of any age are not saved solely by what Jesus did on the cross, or all humans would already be saved. There would now be no sin. We'd all be saved already. With us doing nothing about righteousness or wrong. There would be NO sin! But the Bible says there IS sin, and that there is a Savior. A needed Savior!

THREE WITNESSES AGREE–1ST WITNESS.

I summon three witnesses to support the theory that in order to experience the new birth of water and spirit any sinner must both trust Jesus *and obey Jesus.* By free choice we individually choose our own spiritual leader(s) to follow. As he writes to warn of the fate of those who do not make Jesus their Lord, hear the apostle Paul, witness #1,

> [5] This is evidence of the righteous judgment of God, ... when the Lord Jesus is revealed from heaven with his mighty angels in flaming fire, *inflicting vengeance on those who do not know God and on those who do not* ***OBEY the gospel*** *of our Lord Jesus.* They will suffer the punishment of eternal destruction, away from the presence of the Lord and from the glory of his might ... (2 Thessalonians 1:5-10—ESV, emphasis added).

The apostle affirms that those who do NOT OBEY the gospel will be eternally sorry. If Jesus is Lord, should we not follow and obey Him? Paul's words make it clear that sinners are called on to DO something in order to be saved. God invites us to not only trust Jesus, but to also OBEY Him in order to live. Rejecting is fatal. What the gospel offers is life-giving. It's important. It's essential. *We can be saved by rejecting sin and obeying Jesus!*

That's witness #1, clear and concise. Because of what Jesus did on the cross, salvation is available for every human. But we must choose to obey the risen Lord. We must turn away from sin. The "good news" of His death on Calvary and the resurrection of Jesus is "the gospel." Sinners are saved only if each believes and is led to OBEY what is called for by the good news that Jesus loves and can save. Do we understand? Do we believe it? Those who obey JESUS live. Those who DO NOT OBEY THE GOSPEL will be eternally lost.

Or is the apostle Paul wrong in saying so? Some disagree with Paul. But Paul tells it like it is. As he also did in Romans 6:19: "You also must consider yourselves dead to sin and alive to God in Christ Jesus."

2ND WITNESS.

Jesus told one man that a new birth must be coupled with what His death makes possible, or else any particular person will NOT be saved. His atoning death was all JESUS needed to do. Now each sinner has something to do if the sinner seeks salvation. Hear Jesus, witness #2: [3] Jesus answered him, "Truly, truly, I say to you, *unless one is born again he cannot see the kingdom of God.* ... unless one is born of water and spirit, he cannot ***enter*** the kingdom of God ..." (John 3:3-5—ESV, emphasis added).

We've heard the testimony of two witnesses. Jesus died for us. He REQUIRES a new birth of water and spirit. Only those who in obedience to the gospel are spiritually reborn will be saved by what Jesus did on the cross. Being raised into NEW LIFE must follow a new birth of water and spirit! "You also must consider yourselves dead to sin and alive to God in Christ Jesus." Paul and Jesus both know this and say so.

That's #1 and #2. The message of the cross draws ALL. Only SOME hear and obey the gospel, having chosen to enter. Others hear and reject God's call and are lost. If Jesus did it all, then every sinner is saved at birth—no NEW birth needed! Who dares to say Jesus was wrong? Some bravely do, and some seem to know nothing of the new birth of water and spirit Jesus says is preparatory to being RAISED *INTO* NEW LIFE.

3RD WITNESS.

Witness #3 holds the keys to Christ's kingdom. Peter, apostle of Jesus Christ, invites sinners to repent and be baptized in order to receive remission of sins. His invitation to sinners is not, "Come join us because what Jesus did on the cross has already saved you." Hear the apostle Peter:

> [36] "... 'Let all the house of Israel therefore know for certain that God has made him both Lord and Christ, this Jesus whom you crucified.' Now when they heard this they were cut to the heart, and said to Peter and the rest of the apostles, 'Brothers, what shall we do?' And Peter said to them, 'Repent and be baptized every one of you in the name of Jesus Christ for the forgiveness of your sins, and you will receive the gift of the Holy Spirit. For *the promise is for you and for your children and for all who are far off,* everyone whom the Lord our God calls to himself.' And with many other words he bore witness and continued to exhort them, saying, '*Save yourselves* from this crooked generation.' So those who received his word were baptized,

and there were added that day about three thousand souls" (Acts 2:36-41—ESV, emphasis added).

Think of these three ancient writings as they relate to one another. Within the last year or so of His ministry, Jesus spoke with Nicodemus about the coming kingdom. That was first of these three. It was prophetic. The kingdom was promised but had not yet come upon the earth. It was to come later. Jesus said that when His Kingdom had begun, entrance was *only* by way of a new birth of water and spirit.

Birth Follows Conception.

Some think conception which leads to new birth is by the Holy Spirit. Jesus is uniquely God's Son because HE was conceived within Mary by the Spirit. If all Christians were conceived by the Spirit, would not Jesus cease to BE the UNIQUE Son of God?

Since the Word makes clear that it's by sinners hearing the gospel that faith comes, then I think we should believe that *faith comes by hearing the gospel* (Romans 10:17) rather than by some mysterious "work of the Spirit" not spoken of in any related conversion experience in the apostolic age.

Jesus is God's Word—creator of all life. Another was inspired to write concerning the new birth: "Every good gift and every perfect gift is from above, coming down from the Father of lights with whom there is no variation or shadow due to change. Of his own will he brought us forth *by the word of truth,* that we should be a kind of firstfruits of his creation" (James 1:17,18—ESV, emphasis added).

Paul had said, "You also must consider yourselves dead to sin and alive to God in Christ Jesus." I hear James affirming that JESUS saves and that belief in and obedience to His Word of truth (His gospel) brings us into new life. This is explained more fully later in this study. Here you will read what the bible says about how sinners were and are *RAISED INTO new life with Christ.*

***

INTRODUCTION

More than three years before disciples of Christ were by Jesus commissioned to invite new disciples into the Jesus Way, a cousin of Jesus of Nazareth had begun preaching "in the wilderness" in Judea. Judea was where most "Jews" lived. Called "John the Baptist," he began baptizing God's people, "Jews," who had come to hear John and who wanted to please God and participate in the promised kingdom.

The message John proclaimed prior to baptizing his repentant Jewish hearers was that a promised new kingdom was "at hand." In preparation for that kingdom, all Jews were called to repent of sin and be baptized. Jews, he said, were to return to the ways taught by God through Moses and God's prophets of old. Those who did repent were immersed in water. All who accepted John's baptism were likely candidates to soon afterward enter the promised kingdom.

John's baptism of his fellow Jews featured as essential factors: 1) a call to repentance, 2) a promise of forgiveness for past sins, and 3) preparation for God's soon-to-come earthly kingdom. Baptism associated John's followers with his program of preparation for the Messiah through repentance. He had no group or institution for them to join. This is the case also with baptisms performed by disciples of Jesus Himself prior to His ascension back into heaven. Whether performed by John's disciples or by disciples of Jesus, these were Baptist baptisms of repentant Jews anticipating a *future* kingdom. The kingdom was first opened to membership on the day Jesus baptized His apostles in His Spirit (Acts 2).

There was no *organization* of Jews baptized by John and readying for the kingdom. As individuals, each was PREPARING for the coming kingdom which we call Christ's "church." The church is really an *assembly*, which is what the Greek word means. And it is a separated and organized group, all loyal to the one king and lord, Jesus. These baptized Jews, however, did not form a church! The church was a *future* promise. It was after this that Jesus said, "I WILL build my church."

As a faithful Jew, Jesus was among those who responded to John's call for Jews to be baptized. Yet John realized that Jesus was different from every other respondent. Jesus had no sin. Jesus needed no repentance and remission of sin. So John did not want to baptize Him. However, Jesus insisted on the baptism since all faithful Jews had received God's call in that day to come to John and be baptized. And Jesus was in every respect a faithful Jew! He kept the law of Moses perfectly. He acted always as His Father directed.

The aim in this study is to point out some of the things in the bible which make clear what is accomplished when sinners die to sin, are buried, and are then RAISED INTO NEW LIFE. Every instance (recital) of conversion to Christ recorded in the bible is found in the New Testament book of Acts. That's where we look for examples of sinners becoming saints. What worked then might be expected to work now as it did then. Some choose to ignore the examples and search until they find verses elsewhere which might be used to suppose that other ways bring sinners into Christ's kingdom. Surely it's wiser to see how conversion occurred in the apostolic age rather than to search for some other way. Only we now who *obey the gospel* will be saved by what Jesus "already did on the cross." That's how it was done then. That's how it must be done now.

Being raised into new life follows burying the old man of sin. Being buried and raised is closely linked with our first really hearing the gospel, believing it applies to us personally, and turning away from sin. Can unrepentant sinners save themselves? Paul wrote to Christians in Rome, "You also must consider yourselves dead to sin and alive to God in Christ Jesus." Can anyone other than Jesus save from sin? Jesus and Paul agree that *dying to sin* must precede being raised into new life.

The apostle says that men of any age save themselves by "obeying the gospel." Something is required of seeking and asking in order to receive cleansing by the blood of Jesus. In this study I point out the minimum required for "new birth." Perhaps some have in mind passages which might seem to promise salvation prior to completion of the new birth. Many verses point out that faith in Jesus is essential FOR salvation. None promise salvation by faith ALONE. According to Jesus, required also for conversion into Him is NEW BIRTH of water and spirit. Inspired and reported examples of conversion into new life with

Christ in apostolic times are considered in this study. We will point to several Bible passages about conversions to Christ after first inviting consideration of some pre-Christian initiatory and cleansing ceremonies.

Some Background Truths

We're told that in some "mystery" (secretive) religions in the first century, a baptismal ceremony inducted new members into the religion. And many religions included various "washings" aimed at purification from sin. Since their purpose was to cleanse from sin they were similar in some ways to acting in obedience to the Christ to seek salvation in Him. In some cases, "cleansing water" or other material was sprinkled toward (and/or over) persons seeking cleansing. In other cases, the entire person or the person's hands were washed to remove possible contamination.

A practice had sprung up among the Jews whereby non-Jews could convert to the Jewish religion in the first century A.D. by being circumcised and baptized. Jewish proselyte baptism associated the proselyte (any Gentile who converted to the God of the Bible) with Judaism. The purpose of proselyte conversion was to make the converted Gentile a part of the people of God who commonly were called the Jews. These were the community established and perpetuated by faithfulness to the covenant between God and chosen descendents of Abraham.

God's covenants with Abraham, Isaac, and Jacob gave meaning to circumcision as part of the conversion process into God's Jewish family. The converted (circumcised and baptized) Gentile, having become one of God's covenant people, was then said to be dead to his non-Jewish past and origins.

Likewise, it is suggested that to have been "baptized into Moses" committed those freed slaves who crossed the Red Sea to accept Moses as their leader in bringing God's people out of Egyptian bondage. Paul wrote about this:

> [1] I want you to know, brothers, that our fathers were all under the cloud, and all passed through the sea, and all were *baptized into Moses* in the cloud and in the sea ... (1 Corinthians 10:1,2—ESV).

 Instructions, examples, and relevant information about being raised into new life with Christ are found in the New Testament rather than in the Old Testament. Old Testament books were mainly written in the Hebrew language. They teach us nothing about NEW LIFE in Christ. It's in the New Testament writings that we read about Jesus saving sinners. New Testament original writings were in the Koine Greek language. This was the language of the common people in the lands where in the early years of church history these books were written. So they wrote in Greek.

At the time of writing of New Testament books, Rome ruled that part of the world about which we Westerners know (not the Orient or American or Asian or Pacific areas). Yet the language of commerce and learning was that of Greece. Most people could understand at least some Greek words and were apt to be able to make themselves understood by speakers of the Greek language. English came much later.

In particular, our information source for being RAISED INTO NEW LIFE is that part of the Bible which deals with Jesus on earth and His establishing through His apostles of an "assembly" (a church family) for us who would become His disciples. Shouldn't teaching of Bible truths always be in simple words most people might understand?

The plan in this study is to point first to what Jesus taught about the coming kingdom, then to see how the apostles put into practice what they had been taught, then to look to later teaching by the apostles concerning the Way of life into which they had been led. Conclusions then can be drawn based on what is heard from Jesus and His apostles. We believe Jesus inspired and led His apostles into all needed spiritual truth. They put into practice what He taught them. Some today seek to learn from and to obey Jesus as His apostles and early Christians did. I hope that may be the goal of each reader.

***

WHAT JESUS SAID ABOUT BEING RAISED INTO NEW LIFE

John the Baptist had been sent to prepare the way for the kingdom. The time had not yet come for the King to be crowned. It would be soon! Jesus went about doing good, healing and teaching and preparing for His sacrificial death. He did NOT at that time publicly explain how entrance to His kingdom would be possible. He did have His disciples practice baptism—"Baptist baptism" of repentant Jews. He sent His disciples into villages throughout Judea to inform of the coming kingdom, to join His voice with that of His cousin John.

Immersions were performed by John, or by a disciple of John or, later, by a disciple of Jesus. Those who experienced Baptist baptism as repentant Jews expecting a kingdom which would soon come were not aware of Jesus, the King. John made clear that although he baptized in water, the coming King would later baptize in two different elements—in fire, or in the Holy Spirit.

Disciples of the Christ could not and cannot baptize in either fire or the Holy Spirit. Only God could do so. As John did, they immersed converts in water. Yet it was prophesied by His cousin John that Jesus would baptize some in the Holy Spirit, as He did, and some in fire, as He surely will do at the last judgment.

Baptism in the Holy Spirit was to confer particular powers and gifts upon a very few selected persons, or to signal God's acceptance of those baptized in His Spirit. Only a few received baptism in the Spirit. Baptism in fire will be the fate of all who at the final judgment are not found to have become followers of the Way of Christ.

Also, Jesus is quoted in Mark 10:38,39 speaking of a baptism other than John's that He would later experience. It appears that Jesus there spoke of the suffering which He would undergo at Calvary. His apostles were promised that they too would suffer for the sake of the gospel: [38] *Jesus said to them "You do not know what you are asking. Are you able to drink the cup that I drink, or to be baptized with the baptism with which I am baptized?" And they said to him, "We are able." And Jesus said to them, "The cup that I drink you will drink, and with the baptism with which I am baptized, you will be baptized ..."* (Mark 10:38,39—ESV, emphasis added).

Some want it to be that Jesus baptizes every convert with (in) His Spirit. They think that's what the prophecy of John means. Some also think that would fulfill the prophecy Peter quotes in Acts 2. But why would Jesus have commissioned MEN to baptize converts if HE was going to do the job Himself? It can't be doubted that Jesus gave the job of baptizing to MEN to do! *Jesus commands that HUMANS shall baptize new believers.* Matthew reports His commission this way:

> Matthew 28:16-20 [16] Now the eleven disciples went to Galilee, to the mountain to which Jesus had directed them. And when they saw him they worshiped him, ... And Jesus came and said to them, *"All authority in heaven and on earth has been given to me. Go therefore and MAKE DISCIPLES of all nations, BAPTIZING THEM in the name of the Father and of the Son and of the Holy Spirit, TEACHING THEM to observe all that I have commanded you. And behold, I am with you always, to the end of the age"* (Matthew 28:16-20—ESV. Emphasis added).

Once again Jesus has made clear His claim to being God. After His death and resurrection, He claimed that ALL authority had now been placed in His hands. The confusion could end. Now He was giving His friends and followers their marching orders. No longer were they to dream of an earthly kingdom. They, instead, would travel throughout kingdoms of this present world, everywhere telling others about a risen and loving Lord. Their duties then included baptizing those who came to believe in Jesus, and teaching new converts more and more about what Jesus had said and done and now wanted His disciples to do.

Hearing the commission from Jesus, the apostles were caught off balance. Indeed, both confused and off balance they were. But these disciples (apostles) who were with Jesus in Galilee now were convinced that *Jesus* had been RAISED INTO NEW LIFE. His friends and followers had fully expected Him to become a king on this earth when it had never been intended to be so. Only now did they understand, and still they did not completely understand. They all were Jews. They now knew that Jesus had risen from the dead, regardless of how dreadful His death had been. They had seen Him alive again. After he had died, they had heard Him and talked with Him. They had eaten with Him. His resurrection could not be doubted. Yet His future plans were not clear to them. He was not doing what they had planned and dreamed He would do. They were Jews. They wanted Jews to again have an *earthly* kingdom! That had been their dream and hope.

Those to whom Jesus says the gospel is to be taken are "people groups" rather than "nations" as such. Note how Mark tells of the great commission with which Jesus sent forth His apostles: Mark 16:15,16 [15] *And he said to them, "Go into all the world and proclaim the gospel to the whole creation. WHOEVER BELIEVES AND IS BAPTIZED WILL BE SAVED, but whoever does not believe will be condemned"* (Mark 16:15,16—ESV, emphasis added.).

Whoever believes and IS immersed shall be saved. This is the promise of Jesus as the gospel of Mark words the commission. It is suggested by some that Mark may have not written the last few verses of the "gospel according to Mark" as it appears in most English Bibles. We can only report that the text as it is found in several ancient manuscripts does include this wording, which in no way disagrees with other Bible teaching.

The text here uses a word which translates as "proclaim" or "preach" rather than the "make disciples" or "teach" chosen by Matthew in his account of the giving of the commission. Paul uses a form of the same verb in writing that "*God thought (it) good through the folly of the PROCLAMATION to save the believers*" (1 Corinthians 1:21). Cornelius was told by God's messenger that Peter would bring him a message by which he would be saved. It's not just any proclaiming which saves. It's the proclaimed *message of the cross* which saves those who obediently respond to it. The "proclamation which saves" is summarized by the apostle Paul in 1 Corinthians 15:1-8:

> [1] Now I would remind you, brothers, of the gospel I preached to you, which you received, in which you

stand, and *by which you are being saved,* if you hold fast to the word I preached to you, unless you believed in vain. For I delivered to you as of first importance what I also received: that Christ died for our sins in accordance with the Scriptures, that he was buried, that he was raised on the third day in accordance with the Scriptures, and that he appeared to Cephas, then to the twelve. Then he appeared to more than five hundred brothers at one time, most of whom are still alive, though some have fallen asleep. Then he appeared to James, then to all the apostles. Last of all, as to one untimely born, he appeared also to me (1 Corinthians 15:1-8—ESV, emphasis added).

What we are told to tell others, whether in conversation or in writing or in proclamation, is the *gospel* (good news) of Jesus who came to earth to die in place of sinners so that we sinners might have undeserved eternal life. It's as the proclamation about Jesus is read or heard that "gospel seed" which can produce eternal life within sinners is "planted." Only those who HAVE received, then believed, the gospel and who SEEK salvation from sin could ever be baptized, then RAISED INTO NEW LIFE with Christ.

JESUS could have raised an armed rebellion. Discontent was rife throughout the land. He was popular. Taxes and tax-collectors were hated. Soldiers were everywhere present and were feared. Jesus taught. Jesus healed. He paid required taxes. Jesus loved and *taught others to love*. Jewish leaders may have hoped they saw a leader who would free Israel from Roman rule. One of the political leaders came to Jesus privately one evening. The apostle John reports in John 3:1-6:

[1] Now there was a man of the Pharisees named Nicodemus, a ruler of the Jews. This man came to Jesus by night and said to him, "Rabbi, we know that you are a teacher come from God, for no one can do these signs that you do unless God is with him." Jesus answered him, "truly, truly, I say to you, *unless one is born again he cannot see the kingdom of God.*" Nicodemus said to him, "How can a man be born when he is old? Can he enter a second time into his mother's

womb and be born?" Jesus answered, "truly, truly, I say to you, *unless one is born of water and spirit, he cannot enter the kingdom of God.* That which is born of the flesh is flesh, and that which is born of the spirit is spirit." (John 3:1-6—ESV, except that Ray has changed capitals to lower case on two words which for no apparently good reason in ESV and other translations are capitalized. Emphasis added.)

It may be that Nicodemus was seeking an accommodation with Jesus which would combine forces between Jewish leaders and Jesus to make Him king of a rebuilt Jewish political state. If so, Jesus quietly and firmly made clear the impossibility of this situation ever happening. Jesus didn't directly discuss politics. Perhaps Nicodemus had other purposes for his most unusual private visit. Jesus made clear that only those who were "born again" could be citizens of His kingdom. If Nicodemus had supposed all Jews would automatically be citizens of any kingdom ruled by Jesus, he was made aware of his misunderstanding. Only those who were made morally clean (who were wholly dedicated to God) would be within Christ's organization. This may not have been what the politician expected to hear.

Jews, no doubt including Nicodemus, wanted freedom–for Jews. Jesus offers all good things not only to Jews, but to any person who will seek life in Him. The only way to have life in Jesus is to be born again of water and spirit. Jesus made it unmistakably clear. We who study the matter today can also understand that "new birth into Christ's kingdom" is a change brought about in some way by both water AND spirit, and by being buried and RAISED INTO NEW LIFE.

We are aware that some think by mention here of water Jesus refers to human birth. It seems to me that He speaks of a NEW birth of water and spirit rather than an OLD birth of water and a new birth of the spirit. He did not say, "unless one who was born of water is now born of the spirit." NOTE that Jesus contrasts fleshly and spiritual births. I suggest that's OUR fleshly birth and OUR possible spiritual REBIRTH.

***

HOW WERE EARLY DISCIPLES RAISED?

1. ACTS 2:38-40.

(This text is printed on an earlier page). The celebration of Pentecost described in Acts chapter two saw the beginning of Christian experience. Jews from around the known world were assembled in Jerusalem for this particular Jewish feast. Most were probably very aware of the crucifixion of the Galilean pretender to the throne of David. Some of them may have witnessed His death. It is conceivable that some hearing Peter were among the mob who had cried out for Jesus to be crucified.

The Spirit-empowered preaching of Peter employed the best of Jewish logic. This was appropriate since his hearers were Jews. Those present for the Pentecost ceremonies believed in prophecy and its fulfillment. They also realized that Jewish law required the testimony of at least two "witnesses" to confirm any questionable matter. Peter proclaimed as a fact that Jesus of Nazareth fulfilled the Old Testament requirements to identify Him as the Christ. He pointed out that there were many witnesses to fulfillment by Jesus of Nazareth of the prophetic requirements. Therefore, said the apostle, "*Jesus is the promised Messiah.*" To the Jewish mind, anything foretold in Scripture must someday come to pass. If any event were attested to by at least two witnesses, it must be accepted as fact.

Three thousand men that day heard and believed and acted upon Peter's message. Peter brought to their attention that it was some of THEM who were responsible for putting God's man to death. Some then asked the formerly fearful but now-brave spokesman for God what they could do to make right what they had done wrong. Peter's answer was enlightening and encouraging. They could DO something to put right what they had done wrong. And it was something simple. It was a thing anyone could do. It wouldn't cost them more than they could afford in money or time or talents. No priest or sacrament was called for. It required only an internal change of heart and mind, and then submitting to a public ceremony to demonstrate that they now believed in Jesus and now wanted to serve Him.

Acts 2:38 (sinners can receive) is key to understanding what Jesus said as quoted in John 3:3-8 (sinners must be "born again of water and spirit"). Some think they understand the new birth better than Jesus and the apostle Peter did. They don't. Peter was inspired. It was promised to him that he would be led into all truth. He exhorted seekers to repent and be baptized in order to receive remission of sins. Shouldn't we today have the same message for seeking sinners? Or has Jesus revealed a different way to us? *I hope each of us wants to understand apostolic teaching as the early church did.*

Believers Obey And Are Saved

New life in Christ starts by trusting Jesus. Then we obey Him. In order to receive both remission of sins and an unequalled gift of God's Holy Spirit, God's spokesman advised these seekers they need only repent, and then submit to a brief immersion in water. These seekers all were familiar with John's baptism. The action of Christian baptism was the same. The effects were not the same.

The kingdom which John spoke of as coming had now arrived. This NEW baptism required a change of allegiance. Peter is saying those who want to turn to Jesus and be raised into new life must accept HIS goals and make His goals their own. In so saying, the holder of the keys of the Lord's kingdom was explaining that the "new birth" which brings sinners INTO the Way of Christ includes a spiritual renewal. As was John's baptism, the new birth is of water AND spirit. What's different is the one baptized into Jesus receives within the gift of His Spirit.

That JESUS did and does "pour out" His Spirit is obvious. EVERY convert to Christ RECEIVES the Holy Spirit as a gift as the convert is reborn of water and spirit. *Every* convert. Not just the rich and powerful. Not just the poor and needy. ALL are promised we *will* receive, not baptism in the Spirit, but the "gift of the Holy Spirit Himself." The promise is for all. The prophecy is not fulfilled by continuing baptisms in the Spirit but as an indwelling. Jesus comes to live within each as we are reborn. If we have repented of sin and been baptized into Jesus, through His

 Spirit Jesus walks with us (*in* us) wherever we go in this world! He promised.

Consider what is made clear in inspired writings about some of the acts of Christians in the earliest days of our history. It appears that the normal conversion experience has always been similar to what we read about in Acts 2:38. Men hear the gospel. Some believe it. Some who believe turn away from sin and are baptized into Christ. Others continue in sin.

Those who repent and are baptized receive the promised remission of sins and the almost unbelievable gift of God coming to dwell within them. We move on now to notice other conversions reported by Luke in The Acts, where some of the acts of some in apostolic days are recorded. In Acts we find described only the exceptional conversions. Others are briefly mentioned.

***

2. SOME SAMARITANS (ACTS 8)

When God's people were taken away into Babylonian captivity, the "best" of them were taken—the brave, the beautiful, the useful. The "rest" also had lost their government and their religion with its priesthood and temple. Those left behind built new worship centers. They named new priests. The religion of those who were not taken to Babylon became a mixture. Their bloodlines were no longer based on Abraham, Isaac and Jacob. They were no longer proud to be Jews.

Much later, when a remnant who had survived in Babylon came back to restore Jewish government and religion in Jerusalem, the ones now called Samaritans offered to help rebuild the city and the temple. Their help was refused.

From that time, there was open enmity between "real" Jews and Samaritans. Now however the time has come for Samaritans to hear the gospel. Jesus had told the apostles that they were to witness for Him in Jerusalem first, then nearby in all Judea and in Samaria, and later throughout the world. God sent a strong persecution against the disciples in Jerusalem. They had to flee for their lives. Luke continues the story:

> [4] Now those who were scattered went about preaching the word. Philip went down to the city of Sa-

maria and proclaimed to them the Christ. And the crowds with one accord paid attention to what was being said by Philip when they heard him and saw the signs that he did. For unclean spirits came out of many who were possessed, crying with a loud voice, and many who were paralyzed or lame were healed. So *there was much joy in that city* (Acts 8:4-8—ESV).

Luke informs us that the scattered disciples went every direction fleeing from Jerusalem. He tells of one who chose to go to Samaria. "Signs" given by God through Philip helped convince the people of the city of Samaria that here was something to which they should pay attention. What we learn happened in Samaria took place several months after the gospel of the risen Christ was first preached in Jerusalem. There had been 3,000 converts the first day the church was in existence. Their number soon grew to 5,000, and the growth continued.

All converts during those first thrilling months were Jews. These who were baptized in Samaria were the first who were not fully Jewish who became converts to Christ. Samaritans had once been Jewish, so Samaritans were thought of as part Jewish, and were apparently accepted now with joy as full members of Christ's church.

Simon of Samaria Meets Simon Peter

Then Luke introduces us to Simon of Samaria:

> [9] But there was a man named Simon, who had previously practiced magic in the city and amazed the people of Samaria, saying that he himself was somebody great. They all paid attention to him, from the least to the greatest, saying, "this man is the power of God that is called Great." And they paid attention to him because for a long time he had amazed them with his magic. But when they believed Philip as he preached good news about the kingdom of God and the name of Jesus Christ, they were baptized, both men and women. Even Simon himself believed, and after being baptized he continued with Philip. And seeing signs and great miracles performed, he was amazed (Acts 8:9-13—ESV).

> [14] Now when the apostles at Jerusalem heard that Samaria had received the word of God, they sent to them Peter and John, who came down and prayed for them that they might receive the Holy Spirit, for he had not yet fallen on any of them, but they had only been baptized in the name of the Lord Jesus (Acts 8:14-16—ESV).

Philip's proclamation fell on willing ears. Some Samaritans believed and were baptized. But one of the Samaritans, Simon, enters the picture. From him we learn more about repentance and baptism. As a practicing magician, he wants some of the power he sees being passed on by the apostles. He offers to buy apostolic power. Peter says, "No, that's not the way it's done in the kingdom of Christ." You must repent and pray. So we observe that Christians can make mistakes and be forgiven. Baptism is a one-time event. It can't be repeated. Like human and animal births, baptism is the climax of a spiritual rebirth. No, we can't repeat birth. It happens only once. Then life begins which lasts until the one who was born dies.

Note that the pattern for conversion we saw established in Jerusalem worked somewhat differently this time in Samaria. Luke doesn't mention here that the people who believed and were baptized HAD first repented. I suspect they did, but Luke doesn't say so. And the "gift of the Holy Spirit," Luke seems to say, was lacking until the apostles came from Jerusalem and "laid their hands" upon some of the new Christians. Apostles "laid hands upon" some, who then *were empowered* (as Philip already was by an apostolic anointing) *to perform healings and do other unusual things.*

By reporting that this time the Spirit had not "fallen upon" baptized believers, Luke seems to have meant only that no "special" spiritual powers came to these Samaritans when they were baptized. It's confusing, it seems to me. What is clear is that the gospel was proclaimed and heard, then believed by some. And Samaritans who believed were accepted into the fellowship of Christ's people by being baptized. We do not do well to overlook these similarities, which are common everywhere the gospel was taken in response to the great commission. We can't see it when the "gift of the Spirit" is given to a now-saved sinner. But special power given by the laying on of apostolic hands enabled gifts others could see. That's what Luke reports occurred after the apostles arrived.

***

3. AN ETHIOPIAN (ACTS 8)

[26] Now an angel of the Lord said to Philip, "Rise and go toward the south to the road that goes down from Jerusalem to Gaza." This is a desert place. And he rose and went. And there was an Ethiopian, a eunuch, a court official of Candace, queen of the Ethiopians, who was in charge of all her treasure. He had come to Jerusalem to worship and was returning, seated in his chariot, and he was reading the prophet Isaiah. And the Spirit said to Philip, "Go over and join this chariot." So Philip ran to him and *heard him reading Isaiah the prophet* and asked, "Do you understand what you are reading?" And he said, "How can I, unless someone guides me?" And he invited Philip to come up and sit with him. Now the passage of the Scripture that he was reading was this: *"Like a sheep he was led to the slaughter and like a lamb before its shearer is silent, so he opens not his mouth. In his humiliation justice was denied him. Who can describe his generation? For his life is taken away from the earth."*

[34] And the eunuch said to Philip, "About whom, I ask you, does the prophet say this, about himself or about someone else?" Then Philip opened his mouth, and beginning with this Scripture *he told him the good news about Jesus*. And as they were going along the road they came to some water, and the eunuch said, "See, here is water! What prevents me from being baptized?"

[37] [38] And he commanded the chariot to stop, and they both went down into the water, Philip and the eunuch, and he baptized him. And when they came up out of the water, the Spirit of the Lord carried Philip away, and the eunuch saw him no more, and went on his way rejoicing. But Philip found himself at Azotus, and as he passed through he preached the gospel to all

 the towns until he came to Caesarea (Acts 8:26-40—ESV).

Luke reports that Philip was called away from fruitful proclamation to thousands in Samaria in order to talk to one man. This was an African Jew who had been to Jerusalem to worship in the Jewish temple there, and who was now returning to his home in northern Africa. Ethiopia was the other side of Egypt from Palestine.

This is an example of God intervening to see that one particular person heard the gospel. We suspect He has also done this on other occasions. As the Ethiopian traveled, he was reading. "Books" at that time were scrolls, not simple to read while traveling. We assume this traveler was wealthy. We figure he was not having to drive his own chariot, but that he had at least a driver with him. He was reading from the Old Testament prophet Isaiah. Luke says Philip had been divinely sent there.

Philip introduced himself and asked the traveler if he understood what he was reading. The Ethiopian asked for help to understand. This opened the way for Philip to ride with the Ethiopian for a time and talk with him about Jesus. As they approached a body of water (it's not made clear what branch or creek or pond it was) the Ethiopian asked whether he might be baptized. It seems obvious that Philip had mentioned something to the man about baptism while they talked, and had explained that you couldn't be a disciple of Christ without being baptized. Philip said the man could be baptized if he believed in Jesus, the risen Lord about whom Isaiah had written long years before. So the man who had heard about Jesus, and who now believed in Him and His sacrificial death in place of sinners, was baptized then and there.

We're curious about the church experience which awaited him, since he may have been the only disciple of Christ in Ethiopia when he and his party got home. But that's another story. This story has him hearing and believing the gospel, then obeying it by being baptized. God plans good things for all who hear and obey His Son.

***

4. SAUL OF TARSUS (ACTS CHAPTER 9)

In Acts, Luke tells of the conversion of Saul of Tarsus (yes, we call him the apostle Paul), then later Luke twice recounts Paul's retelling of the story. Here's the record of the first time Paul tells the story:

[1] "Brothers and fathers, hear the defense that I now make before you. ... I am a Jew, born in Tarsus in Cilicia, but brought up in this city [Jerusalem], educated at the feet of Gamaliel according to the strict manner of the law of our fathers, being zealous for God as all of you are this day. I persecuted this Way to the death, binding and delivering to prison both men and women, as the high priest and the whole council of elders can bear me witness. From them I received letters to the brothers, and I journeyed toward Damascus to take those also who were there and bring them in bonds to Jerusalem to be punished.

[6] "As I was on my way and drew near to Damascus, about noon a great light from heaven suddenly shone around me. And I fell to the ground and heard a voice saying to me, 'Saul, Saul, why are you persecuting me?' And I answered, 'Who are you, Lord?' And he said to me, 'I am Jesus of Nazareth, whom you are persecuting.' Now those who were with me saw the light but did not understand the voice of the one who was speaking to me. And I said, 'What shall I do, Lord?' And the Lord said to me, 'Rise, and go into Damascus, and there you will be told all that is appointed for you to do.' And since I could not see because of the brightness of that light, I was led by the hand by those who were with me, and came into Damascus.

[12] "And one Ananias, a devout man according to the law, well spoken of by all the Jews who lived there, came to me, and standing by me said to me, 'Brother Saul, receive your sight.' And at that very hour I received my sight and saw him. And he said, 'The God of our fathers appointed you to know his will, to see the Righteous One and to hear a voice from his mouth; for

> you will be a witness for him to everyone of what you have seen and heard. And now why do you wait? Rise and be baptized and wash away your sins, calling on his name?'" (Acts 22:1-16—ESV, emphasis added).

Yes, here's another exception! This convert had a vision. Jesus appeared to him. He didn't say to Saul, "Now that you've seen me, the risen Lord, you're saved. Now serve me." He didn't say, "You're saved. I died for you." No, Jesus said, "Go on to Damascus. I'll send a man to tell you what you need to do." The man came, restored Saul's sight, told him what he was to later do, then baptized him. That's a shortened form of the story.

In this case, Saul who became Paul already knew the story of Jesus. He just hadn't believed it. Seeing the living man he had thought he knew was now dead changed Saul's understanding of the gospel. He no longer thought the resurrection story foolish and false. Now he knew it was true! He had been vigorously fighting against the Lord's Way. Now he was embracing it.

What a story! So how did he change? When he believed the gospel, he was baptized. Right away when he learned he should do so. That's how it's done. Sinners call on Jesus through obeying the gospel by being baptized as He says any repentant believing sinner should do.

***

5. CORNELIUS & HOUSEHOLD (ACTS 10,11)

Peter explains how he came to baptize a Gentile:

> [1] Now the apostles and the brothers who were throughout Judea heard that the Gentiles also had received the word of God. So when Peter went up to Jerusalem, the circumcision party criticized him, saying, "You went to uncircumcised men and ate with them." But Peter began and explained it to them in order: "I was in the city of Joppa praying, and in a trance I saw a vision, something like a great sheet descending, being let down from heaven by its four corners, and it came down to me. Looking at it closely, I observed animals and beasts of prey and reptiles and birds of the air. And I heard a voice saying to me, 'Rise, Peter; kill and eat.' But I said, 'By no means, Lord; for nothing common or

unclean has ever entered my mouth.' But the voice answered a second time from heaven, 'What God has made clean, do not call common.' This happened three times, and all was drawn up again into heaven.

[11] "And behold, at that very moment three men arrived at the house in which we were, sent to me from Caesarea. And the Spirit told me to go with them, making no distinction. These six brothers also accompanied me, and we entered the man's house. And he told us how he had seen the angel stand in his house and say, 'Send to Joppa and bring Simon who is called Peter; he will declare to you a message by which you will be saved, you and all your household.' As I began to speak, the Holy Spirit fell on them just as on us at the beginning. And I remembered the word of the Lord, how he said, 'John baptized with water, but you will be baptized with the Holy Spirit.' If then God gave the same gift to them as he gave to us when we believed in the Lord Jesus Christ, *who was I that I could stand in God's way?"* (Acts 11:1-17—ESV. Emphasis added.)

HERE'S YET ANOTHER EXCEPTION! This is the first true Gentile we hear of being accepted into the family of God which is Christ's church. Luke tells this story in Acts chapter 10, then has Peter retell it in chapter 11. Cornelius was not a Jew, but he was a godly man, and generous, and good. I earlier mentioned that several miracles were connected with this conversion. It took clear proof to convince Peter that Gentiles were allowed to become disciples of the Jewish Messiah.

Cornelius was visited by an angel who had come to tell him to send for Peter. The angel told him where Peter could be found. This experience would have qualified Cornelius for membership in many "Christian churches" today. But it didn't save Cornelius. Nor would it save anyone. For that's not how Christian conversion occurs. There were miracles. But what saved Cornelius was that as soon as Peter was convinced baptizing a non-Jew was good with God, the repentant, believing Cornelius was baptized. Consider again the story as told by Luke in chapter 10 of Acts:

[1] At Caesarea there was a man named Cornelius, a centurion of what was known as the Italian Cohort, a devout man who feared God with all his household, gave alms generously to the people, and prayed continually to God. About the ninth hour of the day he saw clearly in a vision an angel of God come in and say to him, "Cornelius." And he stared at him in terror and said, "What is it, Lord?"

And he said to him, "Your prayers and your alms have ascended as a memorial before God. And now send men to Joppa and bring one Simon who is called Peter. He is lodging with one Simon, a tanner, whose house is by the seaside." When the angel who spoke to him had departed, he called two of his servants and a devout soldier from among those who attended him, and having related everything to them, he sent them to Joppa.

[9] The next day, as they were on their journey and approaching the city, Peter went up on the housetop about the sixth hour to pray. And he became hungry and wanted something to eat, but while they were preparing it, he fell into a trance and saw the heavens opened and something like a great sheet descending, being let down by its four corners upon the earth. In it were all kinds of animals and reptiles and birds of the air. And there came a voice to him: "Rise, Peter; kill and eat." But Peter said, "By no means, Lord; for I have never eaten anything that is common or unclean." And the voice came to him again a second time, "*What God has made clean, do not call common.*" This happened three times, and the thing was taken up at once to heaven.

[17] Now while Peter was inwardly perplexed as to what the vision that he had seen might mean, behold, the men who were sent by Cornelius, having made inquiry for Simon's house, stood at the gate and called out to ask whether Simon who was called Peter was lodging there. And while Peter was pondering the vision, the Spirit said to him, "Behold, three men are

looking for you. Rise and go down and accompany them without hesitation, for I have sent them." And Peter went down to the men and said, "I am the one you are looking for. What is the reason for your coming?" And they said, "Cornelius, a centurion, an upright and God-fearing man, who is well spoken of by the whole Jewish nation, was directed by a holy angel to send for you to come to his house and to hear what you have to say." So he invited them in to be his guests.

[23] The next day he rose and went away with them, and some of the brothers from Joppa accompanied him. And on the following day they entered Caesarea. Cornelius was expecting them and had called together his relatives and close friends. When Peter entered, Cornelius met him and fell down at his feet and worshiped him. But Peter lifted him up, saying, "Stand up; I too am a man." And as he talked with him, he went in and found many persons gathered. And he said to them, "You yourselves know how unlawful it is for a Jew to associate with or to visit anyone of another nation, but God has shown me that I should not call any person common or unclean. So when I was sent for, I came without objection. I ask then why you sent for me."

[30] And Cornelius said, "Four days ago, about this hour, I was praying in my house at the ninth hour, and behold, a man stood before me in bright clothing and said, 'Cornelius, your prayer has been heard and your alms have been remembered before God. Send therefore to Joppa and ask for Simon who is called Peter. He is lodging in the house of Simon, a tanner, by the sea.' So I sent for you at once, and you have been kind enough to come. Now therefore we are all here in the presence of God to hear all that you have been commanded by the Lord."

[34] So Peter opened his mouth and said: "Truly I understand that God shows no partiality, but in every nation anyone who fears him and does what is right is acceptable to him. As for the word that he sent to Is-

 rael, preaching good news of peace through Jesus Christ (he is Lord of all), you yourselves know what happened throughout all Judea, beginning from Galilee after the baptism that John proclaimed: how God anointed Jesus of Nazareth with the Holy Spirit and with power. He went about doing good and healing all who were oppressed by the devil, for God was with him. And we are witnesses of all that he did both in the country of the Jews and in Jerusalem. They put him to death by hanging him on a tree, but God raised him on the third day and made him to appear, not to all the people but to us who had been chosen by God as witnesses, who ate and drank with him after he rose from the dead. And he commanded us to preach to the people and to testify that he is the one appointed by God to be judge of the living and the dead. To him all the prophets bear witness that everyone who believes in him receives forgiveness of sins through his name."

> [44] While Peter was still saying these things, the Holy Spirit fell on all who heard the word. And the believers from among the circumcised who had come with Peter were amazed, because the gift of the Holy Spirit was poured out even on the Gentiles. For they were hearing them speaking in tongues and extolling God. Then Peter declared, "Can anyone withhold water for baptizing these people, who have received the Holy Spirit just as we have?" And he commanded them to be baptized in the name of Jesus Christ. Then they asked him to remain for some days (Acts 10:1-48—ESV, emphasis added).

Christian baptism in this one case was preceded by careful and powerful preparations which were needed to satisfy Peter and all Jewish Christians that Gentiles could acceptably be baptized into Christ. This Gentile had long wanted to please and serve the true God. Now he could do so, for God had intervened to make it possible, first by providing salvation through His sinless Son, and then by opening the way for Cornelius to learn of Jesus and to obey the gospel by being baptized into Christ.

***

6. A SHAKEN JAILER IS BORN AGAIN (ACTS 16)

Paul and his party came to Philippi. The story is told in Acts 16:11-40. I hope you will read it. Paul and Silas were jailed. God sent an earthquake which opened the jail. The jailer learned of Jesus and His love. He asked, "What must I do to be saved?" Told that salvation was in Jesus, he chose to obey Jesus and live. " ... then they spoke the word of the Lord to him and to all the others in his house. At that hour of the night the jailer took them and washed their wounds. *Then immediately he and all his family were baptized."* (Acts 16:32,33).

Luke, in reporting this event mentions that the new Christians recognized that believing the gospel meant they should obey it by being baptized to begin a life of service for a new Master.

***

We see from examples how conversion of sinner to saint occurs. What we learned is confirmed by teaching of the apostles who were chosen, taught, and empowered by Jesus. Now let's consider what the apostles taught about becoming a babe in Christ. The process by which we are buried with Jesus, then RAISED UP INTO NEW LIFE is exampled. It is also explained in apostolic teaching.

APOSTLES SPEAK ABOUT BEING RAISED INTO NEW LIFE

Readers will note that the gist of being RAISED INTO NEW LIFE is seen in this scripture passage, Romans 6:1-23

> [1] What shall we say then? Are we to continue in sin that grace may abound? By no means! How can we who died to sin still live in it? Do you not know that all of us who have been baptized into Christ Jesus were baptized into his death? We were buried therefore with him by baptism into death, *in order that, just as Christ was raised from the dead by the glory of the Father, we too might walk in newness of life.*
>
> [5] For if we have been united with him in a death like his, we shall certainly be united with him in a resurrection like his. We know that our old self was crucified with him in order that the body of sin might be brought to nothing, so that we would no longer be enslaved to sin. For one who has died has been set free from sin. Now *if we have died with Christ, we believe that we will also live with him.* We know that Christ being raised from the dead will never die again; death no longer has dominion over him. For the death he died he died to sin, once for all, but the life he lives he lives to God. *So you also must consider yourselves dead to sin and alive to God in Christ Jesus. ...*
>
> [20] When you were slaves of sin, you were free in regard to righteousness. But what fruit were you getting at that time from the things of which you are now ashamed? The end of those things is death. But now that you have been set free from sin and have become slaves of God, the fruit you get leads to sanctification and its end, eternal life. For the wages of sin is death, but *the free gift of God is eternal life in Christ Jesus our Lord* (Romans 6:1-23—ESV. Emphasis added.).

The verses omitted above are printed later in this book. We note that Paul was writing this to Christians—to saved sinners, each of whom had already been baptized. Paul was writing to make sure his readers understood the transaction of receiving new birth through repentance and baptism. He speaks of what it had really meant, and what they should do because through new birth of water and spirit they had entered into the Way of Christ.

***

ROMANS 10:8-17

> [8] "The word is near you, in your mouth and in your heart" (that is, the word of faith that we proclaim); because, if you confess with your mouth that Jesus is Lord and believe in your heart that God raised him from the dead, you will be saved. For with the heart one believes and is justified, and with the mouth one confesses and is saved. For the Scripture says, "Everyone who believes in him will not be put to shame." For there is no distinction between Jew and Greek; the same Lord is Lord of all, bestowing his riches on all who call on him. For "everyone who *calls on the name of the Lord* will be saved."
>
> [14] But how are they to call on him in whom they have not believed? And how are they to believe in him of whom they have never heard? And how are they to hear without someone preaching? And how are they to preach unless they are sent? As it is written, "How beautiful are the feet of those who preach the good news!" But they have not all obeyed the gospel. For Isaiah says, "Lord, who has believed what he has heard from us?" So *faith comes from hearing, and hearing through the word of Christ.*

Paul was writing to affirm the necessity of us telling others about Jesus. It's as the gospel is presented that it can be obeyed! Only those who obey the gospel will be made part of the Christian family. Paul is not implying that we need a special class of clergy who will be our "preachers." Every Christian is called to tell others about Jesus. *As the "word" about Jesus is heard, seed is planted which can produce eternal life.*

***

1 CORINTHIANS 1:13-16

> [13] Is Christ divided? Was Paul crucified for you? Or were you baptized in the name of Paul? I thank God that I baptized none of you except Crispus and Gaius, so that no one may say that you were baptized in my name. [I did baptize also the household of Stephanas. Beyond that, I do not know whether I baptized anyone else] (1 Corinthians 1:13-16—ESV).

I hope we all want to understand apostolic teaching as the early church did. Paul calls for us to serve Christ in unity and bases his call for unity on the seven unities he names in Ephesians 4 (quoted later in this study). Foundational to unity is "one baptism." Since Jesus commands baptism for each new believer, the ONE baptism in this age is the baptism commanded by Jesus. Every Christian has entered into life with Christ by way of turning away from sin and then being baptized into Him. And in every case, it's in the same repentant spirit that baptism is done—a spirit of humble obedience, of love, and of confidence in our one Lord.

***

1 CORINTHIANS 10:1-13

> [1] I want you to know, brothers, that our fathers were all under the cloud, and all passed through the sea, and all were *baptized into Moses* in the cloud and in the sea, and all ate the same spiritual food, and all drank the same spiritual drink. For they drank from the spiritual Rock that followed them, and the Rock was Christ. Nevertheless, with most of them God was not pleased, for they were overthrown in the wilderness. Now these things took place as examples for us, that we might not desire evil as they did.
>
> Do not be idolaters as some of them were; as it is written, "the people sat down to eat and drink and rose up to play." We must not indulge in sexual immorality as some of them did, and twenty-three thousand fell in a single day. We must not put Christ to the test, as some of them did and were destroyed by serpents, nor

grumble, as some of them did and were destroyed by the Destroyer.

> [11] Now these things happened to them as an example, but they were written down for our instruction, on whom the end of the ages has come. Therefore let anyone who thinks that he stands take heed lest he fall. No temptation has overtaken you that is not common to man. God is faithful, and he will not let you be tempted beyond your ability, but with the temptation he will also provide the way of escape, that you may be able to endure it (1 Corinthians 10:1-13—ESV).

Whether or not they understood they were doing so, the apostle says those Jewish slaves rescued from Egypt were pledging themselves to follow the leading of Moses. This pledge was sealed, Paul says, as they walked through the sea while being covered by a cloud overhead. Water was above them and all around them as they went into the sea (it was opened before them) and out on the other side. Paul calls this action a "baptism into Moses." A lesson we can learn from Paul's teaching here is that human choices are not irrevocable. Those who were "baptized" that day pledged to faithfully follow Moses as their leader. They didn't stick to that commitment. All of them who were adults on that day died "in the wilderness" without ever entering the promised land. Are we listening? Are we hearing the apostolic lesson? If we have been baptized into Christ, are WE keeping OUR pledge?

***

1 CORINTHIANS 12:12,13

> [12] For just as the body is one and has many members, and all the members of the body, though many, are one body, so it is with Christ. For *in one spirit we were all baptized into one body*—Jews or Greeks, slaves or free—and all were made to drink of one Spirit (1 Corinthians 12:12,13—ESV, emphasis added).

Paul says the baptism which brings us into Christ also brings us into Christ's church, after which we are led to "drink of" God's Holy Spirit (as Peter promised in Acts 2:38). He elsewhere describes our relations with the Spirit as our receiving a "renewal" of the Spirit as we are baptized (Titus 3:5). Every believing repentant sinner is baptized "in the same (human) spirit," that is, in obedience to the common command of our one Lord, Jesus Christ. We are buried with JESUS. We are raised into new life with Him.

It's equal for each one who is baptized into Christ. And as we join ourselves with Christ, we are added by God to His assembly, the Lord's "church" (Acts 2:47). He does not add us to a denomination or even a local congregation. Likely we JOIN with the disciples who meet where we find ourselves. And if we move, or if they move, we will join ourselves with other disciples with whom we can serve our Lord. They will help us and they will receive our help in the work of the Lord.

The church to which God adds us is the timeless assembly of disciples of Christ everywhere in the world and until the end of time. Much as we learn to love our local fellowships, local congregations come and go. A flourishing congregation may grow, or as the years pass it may diminish or die. But Christ's church cannot be defeated. It's the eternal kingdom of Jesus Christ. Those who are made members of the church Jesus built and who continue faithful to Him until the end of their lives or until He returns are sure of eternal life. Paul calls for us to serve Jesus in unity. He bases his call for unity on the seven unities he names in Ephesians 4 (quoted later in this study).

Foundational to unity in Christ is the "one baptism" Jesus commands humans to perform. Every one of us has entered into life with Christ by way of turning away from sin and then being baptized into Him. And in every case, it's in the same spirit that baptism is done—a spirit of humble obedience, of love for, and of confidence in, our one Lord.

Note that we have no vote as to who may join us as members in Christ's body. Every human is welcome to turn to Jesus and find salvation in Him. Each who does so is added to God's church. God has already elected into membership in Christ's "one body" every person who chooses and experiences new birth of water and spirit. This is regardless of any of the distinctives we humans may prefer when we pick our friends.

***

1 CORINTHIANS 15:12-28

[12] Now if Christ is proclaimed as raised from the dead, how can some of you say that there is no resurrection of the dead? But if there is no resurrection of the dead, then not even Christ has been raised. And if Christ has not been raised, then our preaching is in vain and your faith is in vain. We are even found to be misrepresenting God, because we testified about God that he raised Christ, whom he did not raise if it is true that the dead are not raised. For if the dead are not raised, not even Christ has been raised. And if Christ has not been raised, your faith is futile and you are still in your sins. Then those also who have fallen asleep in Christ have perished. If in this life only we have hoped in Christ, we are of all people most to be pitied.

[20] But in fact *Christ has been raised from the dead*, the firstfruits of those who have fallen asleep. For as by a man came death, by a man has come also the resurrection of the dead. For as in Adam all die, so also in Christ shall all be made alive. But each in his own order: Christ the firstfruits, then at his coming those who belong to Christ. Then comes the end, when he delivers the kingdom to God the Father after destroying every rule and every authority and power. For he must reign until he has put all his enemies under his feet. The last enemy to be destroyed is death. For "God has put all things in subjection under his feet." But when it says, "all things are put in subjection," it is plain that he is excepted who put all things in subjection under him. When all things are subjected to him, then the Son himself will also be subjected to him who put all things in subjection under him, that God may be all in all. (1 Corinthians 15:12-28—ESV).

In baptismal waters we who are dying to sin are buried. Death is involved. We choose to be baptized because we choose to put sin to death in our mortal bodies. We opt for baptism because we realize that we are mortal. The death we face impels us to make preparations as best we can for the life we think faces us

 after death. In both these ways death is involved in baptism.
Both death and new life are involved. Out of the waters of baptism we each are raised to walk in NEW LIFE with Jesus Christ.

No person could possibly be baptized for another person. No more could we be baptized for another than we can repent for another or believe for another. Our relationship with our God is personal. There are no ceremonies of any kind which can by themselves change our status with God. God says nothing about "sacraments" which within themselves can affect how God feels toward any individual. There are no payments one can make for the saving of the soul of the one paying, or for another.

But how important it is that we realize that a repentant "man of sin" is being buried in baptismal waters from which a cleansed sinner is raised into new life.

***

2 CORINTHIANS 5:14,15

> [14] For the love of Christ controls us, because we have concluded this: that one has died for all, therefore all have died; and he died for all, that those who live might no longer live for themselves but for him who for their sake died and was raised (2 Corinthians 5:14,15—ESV).

The cross of Christ, when considered in the light of His resurrection, meant that Jesus indeed was dying for the sins of others rather than to atone for any wrongdoing of His own. And this means that we who want to take up His cross and follow Him must also die to sin. In baptism, our repentance is pledged. In repentance and baptism we die to sin and are then raised into new life. Is it not so? We now have entered a new life with Christ. He comes to live in us. We are to forsake sin in order to enjoy life with our sinless Lord!

***

GALATIANS 3:26,27

> [26] ... for in Christ Jesus you are all sons of God, through faith. For *as many of you as were baptized*

into Christ have put on Christ (Galatians 3:26,27—ESV).

This simple apostolic teaching is apparently unknown to many "Christian" people today. For many invite sinners to save themselves by reciting a "sinner's prayer," and then perhaps later be baptized for some reason. I hear the apostle saying simply that faith in Jesus leads us to accept baptism, at which point we become joined to Christ. No one is saved outside the Savior. We who are IN Christ are saved. We "put on Christ" in baptism, says the apostle Paul. We didn't HAVE Him before. That's why baptism is not to be postponed. As soon as any sinner learns of salvation in Jesus and is convinced that Jesus IS the risen Lord who can save from sin, that sinner should be "baptized into Christ." If we believe, will we not obey?

In baptism any repentant sinner can "put on Christ" and be saved. Isn't that what Paul says in this text? Read it again just above. Faith responds to the Lord's command! Isn't that what inspired proclaimers of the gospel that we read about in the Acts always did? There need be no delay. Jesus is willing to save from sin any minute of any day. There'll never be a better time to be baptized than when a sinner first realizes his or her sin and learns how to be saved from the results of having sinned. Paul also points out that we who are in Christ are heirs of God's promise to Abraham, and if we remain in Christ's "one body" we are united.

About the Galatian Controversy

In the Christian Standard for May 18, 2003 is an interesting article by Kevin W. Larsen. It's titled, "Dealing with Theological Differences." This is what the Viewpoint e-mail Discussion group hosted by Ray Downen is aimed at also, of course. Subscribe by sending Ray (now at outreach@sofnet.com) an e-note with the subject, "Subscribe Viewpoint Discussions." I recommend Larsen's article for your inspection. Address of Standard Publishing is 8805 Governor's Hill Dr, Suite 400, Cincinnati OH 45249. I believe every church worker should subscribe to the weekly Christian Standard, and every scholar should subscribe if means permit and access is not certain in nearby libraries. Internet access is also possible.

Larsen speaks of "the controversy in Galatia" in his article. Galatia is the Roman province into which Paul and Barnabas first carried the "gospel to the Gentiles." Paul had enemies before he became a Christian. He had enemies after he became a Christian. He was preaching primarily to Gentiles in Galatia. He first in every city went to the Jewish synagogue so that the gospel could be heard first by faithful Jews. Of all possible hearers, god-fearing Jews should have been the best prospects for becoming Christians. This is still true. But when opposition to the gospel prevented Paul's continued teaching in the synagogue, he took with him those who had accepted the gospel as true and began teaching in non-synagogue locations.

Converts into Jewry needed to be circumcised and only then could be baptized into the Jewish faith and practice. Converts to Christ, according to Paul, did not need to be circumcised, but did need to be baptized. In the earliest years of the church, the gospel was only taken to those who WERE Jews, and therefore to ones who had already been circumcised and who had thereby pledged to obey the Law of Moses. Many Christians assumed incorrectly that before a person could become a Christian he must first, by being circumcised, "become a Jew" as Jesus was.

Paul's accepting into Christ Gentiles who had NOT been circumcised upset some of the Jewish Christians. They felt Paul was wrong. So into each of the new churches which had been established by Paul and Barnabas in Galatia later came other teachers with a "different gospel" than that which had won these converts to Christ. These present enemies of Paul were convinced that circumcision was essential for every Christian, and that every Christian must adopt Jewish customs and traditions in order to adequately be saved and then serve Christ.

Paul respected the Old Testament scriptures which included laws which had been given to God's people by God Himself and by ones inspired BY God to transmit His decrees to His people. Paul taught that these Old Testament scriptures should lead every reader to the Christ toward whom they pointed as a promised "Messiah." Paul taught that sinners were not (could not possibly be) saved by keeping laws, even the perfect law of God. His message was that salvation was found in Jesus Christ and the Way He taught. Circumcision and keeping the Law given by

Moses was not (and of course IS not) any part of becoming a Christian or living as a Christian.

Larsen suggests, "Paul taught that the law's purpose is not for acquiring salvation, but as a tutor to lead one to Christ (Galatians 3:24). One gains salvation [Paul taught, according to Larsen] only by accepting it as a gift offered by God and paid for by the blood of His Son (Romans 5:9)."

This particular way of summarizing the gospel taught by Paul seems to me to be easily misunderstood. It may seem to imply that Paul taught that all it takes to be saved is to do nothing and just let it happen, that somehow the sinner is transformed into a saint while doing nothing. But that's not what Paul taught.

He did teach that sinners need not be circumcised. He did teach that saints or sinners should not try to earn salvation by law-keeping (an impossible endeavor). But Paul does not and did not teach that it was possible to become a Christian by passively waiting and doing nothing. Merely "accepting salvation as a gift" is not within the scope of accurate presentation of the gospel. Sinners are called to OBEY the gospel.

We earlier quoted 2 Thessalonians 1:1-10 where Paul pointed out to brothers in Thessalonica that part of becoming a Christian is OBEYING the gospel—that is, by actively doing something. What Paul taught and what his enemies opposed was that everyone, whether Jew or Gentile, could be saved without trying to earn salvation by keeping laws, without "earning" it by the person's own righteousness. Yet the person must *obey* the gospel by repenting and being baptized!

Larsen surely is right that sinners come to Christ and are saved by what Jesus did on our behalf and by their recognition that salvation is IN CHRIST. If we turn to Christ for salvation we will, without fail, be baptized INTO Him and thereby have our sins washed away. Christ's blood cleanses. Peter had said so. Paul concurs. If obeying called for no action, would Paul have pointed out in this very letter to saints in Galatian churches that sinners are baptized INTO Christ and in being baptized "put on" (clothe themselves with) Christ?

No, Paul clearly taught that our accepting baptism was a part of "*accepting* the gift from God." Paul taught his converts that it's in baptism that we come into Christ. His enemies in those early days were insisting that this was true only if the convert were first converted to the Jewish faith, which included keeping the Mosaic Law.

I think this is not made clear by the wording used by Larsen in this one sentence. Becoming a Christian is done by *doing something* rather than by doing nothing. It involves making a choice between competing agendas. It is done by deliberately turning away from false hopes. It requires moving toward the Savior. Does Jesus save people who do not knock on salvation's door, who do not seek salvation, or who do not ask for what is freely offered? Salvation is not forced upon unwilling victims who only passively accept what must be. It is given to persons who strongly DESIRE and willingly SEEK what is offered. So I don't like the wording, "One gains salvation only by accepting it as a gift."

Yes, of course it IS a gift. No one can earn it, but to receive it, any person must eagerly and sincerely WANT it enough to repent and be baptized in order to be reborn of water and spirit. Those are saved who *obey* the gospel. The Galatian controversy was between those who believed that the Jesus Way included being circumcised and those who denied that circumcision was any part of the Christian Way. In his article Larsen does make this truth clear. So it's only the one sentence which to me seems less clear than it might be that salvation is never by faith alone.

The article is well worth our consideration. Larsen is rightly pointing out that if we're going to contend for "the faith" we need first to know what IS the faith revealed through Jesus and His apostles. For what is revealed, we certainly should contend. For most of the things which we are contentious about, we would do well to love one another and realize that men have no business speaking authoritatively in any matter about which God has NOT spoken. Larsen urges us to weigh the importance of anything about which we want to contend, and avoid fighting about matters which are unimportant. And he urges that in all our work for God that we keep the "right" attitude. He wants us to keep lines of communication open with all who as we do seek unity in Christ. That seems to me to be excellent advice! Jesus wants us to be ONE body. If we all are loving and serving the ONE Lord, shouldn't we be united?

***

EPHESIANS 1:13

"In him you also, when you heard the word of truth, the gospel of your salvation, and believed in him, were sealed with the promised Holy Spirit."

Paul makes clear his knowledge that those who truly believe in Jesus will OBEY Him. He does not here teach that the Spirit is given upon faith alone. The sinner who repents and accepts baptism into Christ is promised that Jesus will THEN take up residence in that person. God's Spirit is His breath. God's "breath" is shared with each newborn Christian!

Those who assist at human birth eagerly await the first breath taken by the newborn. The apostle Peter, speaking for Jesus, promises that the Spirit (breath) of God will without fail be given to every sinner who repents and IS baptized. In the new birth as in every natural human birth, first breath follows the birth.

No "spirits" are involved in salvation prior to the completion of the new birth of water and the one HUMAN spirit which is fully described in this book just as it's described in God's book. Jesus told HUMANS to teach and preach, to carry gospel truth to others, and to baptize those who believe. The Lord Jesus offers eternal life to all who will turn to Him in repentance and then accept the baptism in water by which "new birth" is publicly accomplished and proclaimed. God's "breath" (His Spirit) is gifted to every newly-elected child of God as the cleansed new Christian is RAISED INTO NEW LIFE.

***

EPHESIANS 2:1-10

[1] And you were dead in the trespasses and sins in which you once walked, following the course of this world, following the prince of the power of the air, the spirit that is now at work in the sons of disobedience —among whom we all once lived in the passions of our

 flesh, carrying out the desires of the body and the mind, and were by nature children of wrath, like the rest of mankind. But God, being rich in mercy, because of the great love with which he loved us, even when we were dead in our trespasses, made us alive together with Christ—by grace you have been saved—and raised us up with him and seated us with him in the heavenly places in Christ Jesus, so that in the coming ages he might show the immeasurable riches of his grace in kindness toward us in Christ Jesus. For by grace you have been saved through faith. And this is not your own doing; it is the gift of God, not a result of works, so that no one may boast. For we are his workmanship, *created in Christ Jesus for good works,* which God prepared beforehand, that we should walk in them (Ephesians 2:1-10—ESV, emphasis added).

It's God's GRACE that is His "gift" to us—unearned, a totally undeserved opportunity to trust Jesus and obey Him and receive eternal LIFE. Some suppose that human faith is "the gift of God." No, not at all. In writing to Roman Christians, (Romans 10:1-17) Paul has made clear how faith "comes" to anyone. It's by hearing (or reading) and understanding the inspired writings, particularly the gospel which tells of God's love and the work of Jesus on earth. Notice especially verse 17 of Romans 10.

Paul makes clear that we do not deserve the good things God gives us, including eternal life through Jesus. We haven't earned God's gifts. We can't earn them. God wants us to realize that nothing we do could put Him in our debt. Because God loves us, He offers us eternal life as a gift. If God then expects us to "walk in good works," why would anyone think it doesn't matter how we live? Some suppose all it takes to be saved is to believe in Jesus. They think God does it all, if the sinner just believes something about Jesus.

But there is a spirit at work in God's world which is at enmity with God and with goodness. Some people are controlled by that wicked spirit. These "worldly" people, whether in or outside the church, are disobedient to God. They do not seek to do His will. They want their own way at any cost. Expecting Jesus to have done and be doing all needed for our salvation is to totally misunderstand God's call to action. We are incited to act. We should trust and OBEY JESUS!

Ephesians 2:10 should make clear to every reader that human response to the gospel (a change of intent and purpose) is essential for salvation. God's gift of eternal life is given to those who repent and are baptized, and who then live and love as did Jesus. We who have died to sin will now be living for God. we'll be doing the good works "prepared beforehand" with which God wants us to busy ourselves on this earth. If we love Jesus, we will "keep" His commandments. Christians have repented of self-love. We have chosen to become servants of God to do HIS will.

When we love Him most of all, and obey Him, *Jesus, God's gracious gift to this world, can save us.* His plan is that we will turn away from self-will in order to do His will. Those who love self more than they love God will not be saved from sin. Those who follow fleshly desires are lovers of *self,* and obviously are not in fact spiritually reborn.

***

EPHESIANS 4:1-6

> [1] I therefore, a prisoner for the Lord, urge you to walk in a manner worthy of the calling to which you have been called, with all humility and gentleness, with patience, bearing with one another in love, eager to maintain the unity of the Spirit in the bond of peace. There is one body and one Spirit—just as you were called to the one hope that belongs to your call—one Lord, one faith, *one baptism,* one God and Father of all, who is over all and through all and in all (Ephesians 4:1-6—ESV, emphasis added).

Is not unity a basic, foundational description of the Way of Christ? Paul includes "one baptism" in this listing of the essentials for unity in Christ's church. These are facts, not opinions. The church is built upon these foundations. They're not optional. Ever. Anyone who has experienced Christian baptism has been immersed into DEATH, the atoning death of Christ, and the personal death to sin from which we rise to walk in a changed life-style. After we each "die to sin" in repentance and baptism we then are resurrected to LIVE with Christ and as co-workers with all others who are His.

The "one body" of which Paul speaks is, of course, the assembly Jesus built through His apostles. He adds each of us to His assembly when we are reborn spiritually. We must not seek to split His body apart. It's our job to maintain the body's unity by unswerving loyalty to and service for its one head, who is the one Lord, Jesus Christ.

When we all are loyal to Jesus, will we want to split our loyalty by thinking of ourselves as any kind of Christians at all except LOYAL and loving servants of our one Lord? All who belong to Jesus are Christians. Just Christians. Ones whose loyalty belongs to the Christ, held firmly to Him by bonds of love. We exist to daily and hourly in harmony with our brethren serve our one Lord.

God is one, so of course His Spirit will not say one thing to one disciple and bring a conflicting message to another. God's influence through His one Spirit in His church will bring us together and keep us together. Any thought of splitting the body comes from some source other than our God. We each look forward with longing ... our one hope is for eternal life with our loving Father and His loving Son. Jesus is the one Lord of all. We must remain loyal to HIM and love and serve Him.

The "one faith" which was "once for all delivered" to us can be found described in the written Word which is the New Testament. God's gifts are perfect. The New Testament scriptures need no updating. They need no change. They only need to be believed and obeyed. And they tell us of the one baptism which brings us into the one body. Of course this is the baptism commanded by our one Lord to be performed by His disciples.

Each part of this unity comes from the one God who is in fact three in one, described by Jesus as "the Father, the Son, and the Holy Spirit." The Lord's real prayer (John 17) is that we disciples should seek as perfect unity together as that which exists between God's unique Son and His Father. And they are one.

If our chief aim in life is to please Jesus, then we will do all we humanly can do to be a friend to every other Christian. Yes, we'll see some things differently. we'll not each be exactly like every other child of God. But we will be ONE in spirit and in love and in obedience to our ONE Lord. Our boss has no office on earth. Had we all noticed?

***

EPHESIANS 5:22-33

> [22] Wives, submit to your own husbands, as to the Lord. For the husband is the head of the wife even as Christ is the head of the church, his body, and is himself its Savior. Now as the church submits to Christ, so also wives should submit in everything to their husbands.
>
> [25] Husbands, love your wives, as Christ loved the church and gave himself up for her, that he might sanctify her, having cleansed her by the washing of water with the word, so that he might present the church to himself in splendor, without spot or wrinkle or any such thing, that she might be holy and without blemish. In the same way husbands should love their wives as their own bodies. He who loves his wife loves himself. For no one ever hated his own flesh, but nourishes and cherishes it, just as Christ does the church, because we are members of his body. "Therefore a man shall leave his father and mother and hold fast to his wife, and the two shall become one flesh." This mystery is profound, and I am saying that it refers to Christ and the church. However, let each one of you love his wife as himself, and let the wife see that she respects her husband (Ephesians 5:22-33—ESV, emphasis added).

Paul says that Jesus is Lord of all. He is the HEAD of the church which is His body. We are His church. He owns us. He controls us all. Because we all love and obey Jesus as our Lord we are one body. As "members" of His body, we seek the good of the body, which includes our humbly working together with every other part. Shall we not pray and work for unity in Christ's church of which we each are a part? Later, we will speak of how life-giving seed leads to sinners being cleansed from sin.

***

COLOSSIANS 2:6-15

> Therefore, as you received Christ Jesus the Lord, so walk in him, rooted and built up in him and established in the faith, just as you were taught, abounding in thanksgiving. See to it that no one takes you captive by philosophy and empty deceit, according to human tradition, according to the elemental spirits of the world, and not according to Christ.
>
> For in him the whole fullness of deity dwells bodily, and you have been filled in him, who is the head of all rule and authority. In him also you were circumcised with a circumcision made without hands, by putting off the body of the flesh, by the circumcision of Christ, *having been buried with him in baptism, in which you were also raised with him through faith in the powerful working of God, who raised him from the dead.*
>
> And you, who were dead in your trespasses and the uncircumcision of your flesh, God made alive together with him, having forgiven us all our trespasses, by canceling the record of debt that stood against us with its legal demands. This he set aside, nailing it to the cross. He disarmed the rulers and authorities and put them to open shame, by triumphing over them in him (Colossians 2:6-15—ESV, emphasis added).

Paul reminds that the early church was taught what they should believe. "The faith" was not being developed by men. It was delivered from the mind of God. We today should remain loyal to what the Lord's apostles once for all "delivered" to the early church. We cannot improve on God's revelation. Why do we sometimes try to do so? This body of "faith" which came from God tells us how we should think, talk, and act. So Paul pleads with his hearers that they (and we) should "walk" as God has taught us to do. That is, our daily way of life should be patterned after that of the Lord Jesus. He loved. We love.

And in what are we taught to abound? It's in *thanksgiving.* We need never fret. We should in all things give thanks to our loving Father. We also need to carefully remember what the apostles did teach. We should not seek to change it. We should believe it's true even if it sometimes seems difficult for us to understand.

All the blessings Paul lists as belonging to us who are in Christ are based on our having been born again of water and spirit. Please read this passage again and again and realize Paul is here explaining the PURPOSE of NEW LIFE in Christ. He's talking about what really happened when we obeyed the gospel. Do we NOW know what happened to us when we were buried with Christ in baptism and raised then to walk in NEW life? In baptism we were united with the burial and resurrection of Jesus. God gave us new life after we had died to sin!

***

TITUS 3:5-7

> [5] ... he saved us, not because of works done by us in righteousness, but according to his own mercy, by the washing of REGENERATION [new birth], and renewal of the Holy Spirit, whom he poured out on us richly through Jesus Christ our Savior, so that being justified by his grace we might become heirs according to the hope of eternal life (Titus 3:5-7—ESV, with an addition & emphasis).

Some find in these words a statement that the Holy Spirit saves sinners. But the Spirit is *given by Jesus* to newly reborn children of God. It's not the Spirit giving us Jesus. Just the reverse. Is it possible that children are born with no sin, so that renewal of God's presence within us fits in perfectly with our new birth? Note that the Spirit is the *gift,* not the giver! The giver is Jesus! Peter promises that we who obey the gospel will be gifted by receiving the Spirit, that is, by JESUS coming to live within us. Paul is not saying that it's the Spirit who brings us renewal! JESUS gives the Spirit. We understand the Spirit best when we know *Jesus* best. These exhortations to his friend Titus are another way of saying what Paul has written in Ephesians 2:4-10 quoted earlier in this study.

That is, God saves us in new birth because He loves us, not because we're already or in the future will be marvelous or beautiful or wise or rich or generous. He saves us because of Who He is rather than because of any merit within us. God saves us IN CHRIST through the process of a new birth of water and the (human) spirit which results in His placing His Spirit within us. Our God indeed is gracious, giving us far more than we deserve or could possibly earn. He saves us through the CHRIST and His atoning death on Calvary. Where does baptism fit into this picture? That's easy. It's the culmination of the new birth, the actual birthing of a new life in Christ. Repentance and baptism are "the washing of regeneration" here spoken of. Regeneration is being born again. Jesus says the new birth is of water and spirit.

So how does the Spirit fit into the picture? The Spirit is God's gracious gift to each newly-born Christian. His tasks? To comfort and strengthen us in every way possible that does not take away our freedom of choice; to help us build up our brethren in Christ's body; and to encourage us in our desire to serve the Lord in the ways most pleasing to Him. Through their Spirit, both the Father and the Son dwell within us wherever in the world we may scatter as we seek to serve Jesus and do what is right for ourselves and our loved ones.

We do well to remember, however, that God does not promise to miraculously remind US of what Jesus said, as Jesus did promise would be the case with the apostles who heard Jesus speak. God does not promise to lead US into all truth, as He divinely led apostles and prophets in knowing truth and teaching the church in its early days.

The Spirit was active indeed in the lives of early Christians. In those days, some disciples spoke to the churches through the direct inspiration of God's Spirit. Many sick were miraculously healed. As earlier quoted, Mark's gospel speaks of unusual miracles which would and did in those days accompany the preaching of the gospel.

Most of us in this generation do not see frequent miracles as we daily serve our Savior. Yet some say they do. We can be sure that God is not dead. His Spirit is still walking WITH (within) US. In every need, we do well to call on God. He can and will both lead and strengthen us in whatever ways He chooses to use.

And He works on earth today through His Spirit. Paul reminds Titus of this true fact.

***

HEBREWS CHAPTERS 5 AND 6

Please thoughtfully read what is written in your Bible in these two chapters. Note especially 5:9: *"And being made perfect, he (Jesus) became the source of eternal salvation to all who obey him ..."* And 5:14: *"But solid food is for the mature, for those who have their powers of discernment trained by constant practice to distinguish good from evil."*

And 6:4-6: *"For it is impossible, in the case of those who have once been enlightened, who have tasted the heavenly gift, and have shared in the Holy Spirit, and have tasted the goodness of the word of God and the powers of the age to come, and then have fallen away, to restore them again to repentance, since they are crucifying once again the Son of God to their own harm and holding him up to contempt."*

***

HEBREWS 10:19-26

> [19] Therefore, brothers, since we have confidence to enter the holy places by the blood of Jesus, by the new and living way that he opened for us through the curtain, that is, through his flesh, and since we have a great priest over the house of God, let us draw near with a true heart in full assurance of faith, with our hearts sprinkled clean from an evil conscience and *our bodies washed with pure water*. Let us hold fast the confession of our hope without wavering, for he who promised is faithful. And let us consider how to stir up one another to love and good works, not neglecting to meet together, as is the habit of some, but encouraging one another, and all the more as you see the Day drawing near. For if we go on sinning deliberately after receiving the knowledge of the truth, there no longer remains a sacrifice for sins ... (Hebrews 10:19-26—ESV).

Some Bible teachers think it was Paul who wrote Hebrews. Some are convinced it was not Paul. Does it matter? I think not. The early church felt the book of Hebrews reflected apostolic doctrine. I figure they were in a better position to judge the matter than anyone who has lived since their time could possibly do it.

For whatever reason, God set up a system by which only blood could atone for sin. And not just any blood would do. It must be the guiltless which would atone for the guilty. So in the final analysis, only if God furnished a sinless sacrifice could human sin be atoned for. God provided. The blood of Jesus can wash away sin. But how do we access His blood? It's through a washing with "pure water."

In fact, any water, clean or dirty, frigid or hot or comfortable, running or stagnant—any water at all will do for Christian baptism. For the purity is in the death of Jesus on the cross. His sacrifice makes baptismal water "pure." *Baptism,* the seeking of a clean conscience because it's God's plan for taking sin away, *surely will result in our gaining a clean conscience.* In obeying the gospel, we can be sure we have pleased the author and planner OF that good news. It's baptism that takes away the sin of each repentant believer in Jesus Christ. We've tried to "prove" this by the bible texts previously furnished in this study. It is hoped that they have done the job satisfactorily.

This text also points out that sin is still a possibility for ones who have been washed in the blood of the Lamb of God. And some, using the freedom of choice which God gives each of us, will turn back to sinful ways. Such renegades deserve death, and that's exactly what they will receive unless they repent. God points out that some who once were saved are later so rebellious that their hardened hearts are not responsive to any call for repentance. Some will sin and repent of their sin and be forgiven. Some will not repent. There is no greater sacrifice for sins than Jesus on the cross. Those who spurn salvation through the cross of Christ have no hope of salvation or eternal life.

Why should Christians meet together? The inspired writer speaks of God's plan for our spiritual security. Why did our Lord create an assembly, a family of faith? Some say it was so people would worship Him, and frequently remind Him how good He is and how much they love Him. So they meet frequently so they can worship Him together "in church." But what this text (... let us consider how to stir up one another to love and good works, not neglecting to meet together, as is the habit of some, but encouraging one another ...), and each bible passage on the subject, calls for us to do as we meet together is to build up other Christians, and to receive encouragement from other Christians.

Do we now see that this text is aimed at us strengthening and encouraging Christians as we meet together? Think about it. Watching talented "performers" may not really edify a Christian audience. Friends talking with friends is often edifying. We also may be edified by listening to God's Word read and explained.

It's in HEAVEN that we'll busy ourselves with praise, if we can believe the Revelation. Is there any Bible verse or passage which calls for Christian priests to ever be "led in worship" here on earth? Shall we remember that every Christian is a priest. Time invested in priests "praising God together" in worship assemblies may prevent our being busy doing what Christians are called TO do.

Here on earth His work for us is that we are to love our neighbor no less than we love our self, and to show that love by our actions. We should seek to do good things for others, particularly those whose needs are great. The work we're called to do on earth is to tell others about Jesus. Isn't that what the Bible says? And, as the passage encourages, we want to think well of the church of which we're members. The purpose of the communion (the Lord's Supper) which should be a part of each Lord's Day assembly is for us to give due consideration to the needs of all "the body" which on earth is His church.

***

1 PETER 3:15-22

[15] ... but in your hearts regard Christ the Lord as holy, always being prepared to make a defense to anyone who asks you for a reason for the hope that is in you; yet do it with gentleness and respect, having a good conscience, so that, when you are slandered, those who revile your good behavior in Christ may be

 put to shame. For it is better to suffer for doing good, if that should be God's will, than for doing evil.

> [18] For Christ also suffered once for sins, the righteous for the unrighteous, that he might bring us to God, being put to death in the flesh but made alive in the spirit, in which he went and proclaimed to the spirits in prison, because they formerly did not obey, when God's patience waited in the days of Noah, while the ark was being prepared, in which a few, that is, eight persons, were brought safely through water.
>
> BAPTISM, which corresponds to this, NOW SAVES YOU, not as a removal of dirt from the body but as an appeal to God for a good conscience, through the resurrection of Jesus Christ, who has gone into heaven and is at the right hand of God, with angels, authorities, and powers having been subjected to him (1 Peter 3:15-22—ESV).

Peter makes no apology for believing that Christian baptism is involved in salvation. He simply says, "Baptism now saves you." Did Peter believe Jesus saves solely by what He did on Calvary? No, the apostle urged sinners to save themselves by repenting and being baptized. Have we correctly understood Peter then if we think he is teaching that we are saved prior to our baptism into Christ? No. Should we apologize for seeing that the new birth of water and spirit is essential for salvation? No.

Shall we ignore Acts 2:38 in discussing how sinners become saints? We should not. Earlier we called attention to what Peter said at the birthday of the church (Acts chapter two). He exhorted his hearers to save themselves by repenting and being baptized. And as soon as he was convinced that the gospel was for Gentiles as well as Jews, Peter commanded the particular Gentiles in question to be baptized. Even ones who had just enjoyed a unique spiritual blessing were not saved without Christian baptism.

You noticed that the angel told Cornelius that Peter would bring a *message* that would save him. How urgently we need to proclaim that Jesus SAVES. I point out once again that converts were never told they already HAD BEEN saved by what Jesus did on the cross. There was something sinners were required now to DO in order to receive remission of sins. The new birth is of water AND the (human) spirit. A new Christian is one who now believes the gospel so has now repented and accepted baptism in water. Baptism alone is no better than faith alone or repentance alone. The new birth is of water AND spirit.

***

CONCLUSIONS ABOUT OUR BEING RAISED INTO NEW LIFE

Jesus said entrance into His Kingdom was by way of a new birth of water and spirit. When He said this, the kingdom was still future. The kingdom DID come, as reported in chapter two of Acts. Peter, who had been given the "keys to the kingdom," as the church was being born, urged seekers after salvation to do what men must do in order to enter it. Peter's exhortation provides the most easily understood description of the new birth available to Bible readers. Peter's explanation of how to enter the kingdom was that men must repent of sin and must accept baptism into Christ. The sequence is clear. Hearing is first. Believing truth is next. Choosing to act according to truth follows. "You also must consider yourselves dead to sin and alive to God in Christ Jesus." Christ's church is the kingdom ruled by God's unique Son. It's His assembly. We speak of it as His "church."

***

GOD'S WORD IS THE SEED FOR NEW LIFE

The life-giving seed is the gospel story about Jesus of Nazareth. In Ephesians 5:22-33 Paul speaks of how Jesus has "cleansed us (His church) by the washing of water with the word?" We should not imagine the apostle doesn't know the difference between water and "the word." Water is a cleansing agent. Words are not. Our sins are washed away in baptism's waters as we enter the Lord's body which is His "church." Through us hearing or reading of Jesus, God's WORD, and believing the gospel, we were begotten for new birth. In baptism into Him, our sin was washed away. We were raised into new life. We are saved through hearing and believing and then obeying the gospel. We notice that in several passages, it is said that hearers believed when the obvious meaning is they believed and also acted upon their belief.

Christians "sow seed for new birth" by proclaiming the gospel of Christ. We should be diligent to share gospel truth with all with whom we come in contact. God will give the increase. At the time of His choosing. His timing may not agree with ours. What is the life produced by the gospel? It's salvation in Jesus. And sinners who trust in Jesus and obey His gospel by turning away from sin and being baptized into Christ receive the "gift" of the Spirit of Jesus being sent to live IN them. This is identical for every one of us. We were equally sinners, lost apart from Christ. We equally receive the Spirit and new life when we repent and are immersed, then are RAISED INTO NEW LIFE. Faith in JESUS which causes us to obey the Gospel saves us. God is good!

The apostle Paul speaks of the results we may expect from sowing gospel seed. Galatians 3:5 presents the truth as a question, "Does God give you His Spirit ... because you observe the law, or because you believe what you heard?" The expected answer of course is that God's gifts are given to those who believe rather than to those who try to earn them. Paul agrees with Peter who promised believing sinners that if they turned away from sin and were obedient to the gospel by being baptized that they would receive God's gift of life (Acts 2:38). Life-giving seed is the good news about Jesus who is able to save any sinner.

***

WERE YOU ELECTED TO SALVATION?

Jesus explains how the seed which produces "new life" is sown. Those who want "new birth" to be of water and the Holy Spirit should note that the planting of seed which produces new life is not commissioned to be done by the Spirit. It's not DONE by the Spirit. It's done by humans or the written Word presenting a choice to the human spirit. Saving seed is planted by us humans as we carry the gospel throughout the world.

It's like the difference between human birth and a virgin birth. God put in place a "normal" means of human reproduction. No intervention other than interaction between male and female humans is normally needed to effect human birth. "Nature," God's reproductive plan, operates as designed.

Being RAISED INTO NEW LIFE is similar. God does not "elect" particular persons to be saved. He orders that the good news of available salvation is to be taken to ALL. God chose that all who hear or read and obey the gospel shall be saved. He voted. He provides a Way into eternal life. Satan voted. He opposes. Now it's our turn! Some do listen, believe, and act as the gospel directs. Those who do so save themselves. They're voting YES. We individually "elect" ourselves to salvation. Just as with the "law of gravity" which equally affects every person and object on earth or in space, God has put in place the means of salvation. It's provided. It's available. The gospel affects every person equally. We go. We tell. Some hear. Those who obey the gospel are saving themselves.

Those who choose to not believe or who do not obey the gospel remain "elected" to certain eternal death. In Ephesians 1:13, Paul reminds Ephesian Christians that they also "were included in Christ when" they "heard the word of truth, the gospel of your salvation." They heard and believed and, obeying, "were marked in him with a seal, the promised Holy Spirit."

***

WHEN IS THE SPIRIT GIVEN?

Peter (Acts 2:38) says that AT baptism (not before baptism) sinners receive the "gift of the Holy Spirit." Paul (1 Corinthians 12:13) describes this gift of the Spirit as the former sinners being "made to drink of the Spirit." In both cases, this experience is a result of our having already been baptized into Christ. Obviously then, the gift is not baptism itself. Nor is baptism "being made to drink of the Spirit." Both gift and drinking follow baptism and being raised into new life. The scriptures in reference are Acts 2:38 and 1 Corinthians 12:13.

Had you realized that in both cases Christ's apostle makes clear that as Christian baptism took place something has CHANGED? Is it not equally obvious that our interaction with the Spirit FOLLOWS (rather than precedes or in any way causes) our baptism?

 If we understand that the new birth is of water and the human spirit, it's easy to see how Peter's guidance to sinners seeking salvation ties in with the statement earlier made by Jesus that entrance into His kingdom is through both water and spirit. When gospel truths are heard, sinners are welcome to believe them and are ABLE to believe them. This takes no new revelation from God that wasn't present already when the very first ones who heard the gospel cried out to God's spokesman to ask, "What shall WE DO?"

The plan for salvation was in place from the beginning. The plan is from God. It was fulfilled by God's Son who died in place of sinners so that we sinners could receive eternal LIFE. Peter opened the Way. His reply to seekers was simply that they must turn away from sin (turning TO Jesus as their new boss) and that they must be baptized as Jesus had instructed was to be done when someone heard and first believed the gospel. Our hearing the gospel takes no new action by God's Spirit. The facts are clear from long ago. The Spirit's convicting and empowering was fully done in the first Christian century as the truth was proclaimed and recorded. Evangelism happened. Inspired writings were published.

The Spirit's work is being done when people read and teach the writings inspired through Him. Jesus instructed that those who loved Him should make gospel facts known throughout the world. The Spirit is given to help US tell everywhere about *Jesus*. But rather than the Spirit, it's PEOPLE who are told to DO the telling. It's PEOPLE who are told to do the baptizing and raising into new life! The Spirit helps US tell others. He is given to ones who have already repented and have been baptized.

***

JESUS CALLS FOR PEOPLE TO BAPTIZE

PEOPLE are told to immerse (in water of course—what else?) those who hear the gospel and want to join with the risen Lord in living for God. This baptizing is not done by the Spirit. HUMAN hands perform Christian baptism. No divine assistance is required for us to obey the Lord's clear command that we should teach about Jesus to (make disciples of) all people everywhere, then to baptize those hearers who come to believe in the risen Lord, and then to continue teaching the new disciples. No divine assistance is required for sinners to believe what they read or what they hear from us. Both proclaiming and hearing are within our power as humans. It does not take action by the Spirit to let a sinner believe in Jesus. It does not take special spiritual gifts to tell others about Jesus. It doesn't require a college education either to understand or to explain the gospel. We need no human authority and no further divine assistance to tell others about Jesus.

The instructions given by Jesus concerning the baptism He commanded included that the act was to be done "in the name of the Father, Son, and Holy Spirit." Baptism "into Christ" is done by the authority of, in respect and honor for, and to bring each convert into fellowship with God in His entire being. In actual practice, we're told that baptism was actually done "in the name of Jesus," as shorthand for the longer list Jesus gave of the persons who together form our one God, and in recognition of the authority now given to Jesus alone.

Apparently early Christians, and the apostles, did not suppose Jesus in His "great commission" meant to be giving some kind of "proper formula" for someone to say to make baptism valid. If anything is recorded about what was said when a baptism was performed, no reporter in bible times ever speaks of the baptizer using this particular wording. Generally what the report says is only that the person was baptized "in the name of Jesus." It is not John's baptism which now is offered.

Some are troubled by a Bible verse which could mean that it isn't people who are to baptize people who have repented of sin and want to work for Jesus. Jesus said WE were to carry the gospel with us wherever we go and that WE were to baptize each new believer. He knows best. No one goes wrong by obeying Jesus! The apostle Paul is properly understood in 1 Corinthians 12:13 to be speaking of the spirit of humble obedience which was shown by EVERY obedient believer in Jesus as Lord. Calling us to unity, the apostle Paul points out in 1 Corinthians 12:13 that our baptisms are all exactly alike in being an immersion in water from which we are raised into new life. Why? Because we all recognized JESUS as Lord and by accepting baptism we all are submitting to HIS leadership. The same spirit. Submission. Obedience. That's us. EVERY one—all of us.

The apostle is NOT establishing the Holy Spirit as the baptizer! He writes "in ONE spirit we all were baptized into the body of Christ." He's been writing about gifts given through the Holy Spirit. If the apostle had meant the Holy Spirit did the baptizing, surely he would have written, "baptized by THE Spirit ..." rather than baptized "in ONE spirit ..." Wouldn't he? He's not contrasting spirits of which there may be more than one. This subject is considered at greater length in a future companion volume, RAISED INTO NEW LIFE, Part 2. The complete book is simply "Were You RAISED INTO NEW LIFE With Christ?."

The great commission IS directed to humans. And Peter, speaking for the Lord urged HUMANS to add to their faith (2 Peter 1:1-15). He didn't tell us to call on the Spirit to GIVE us these good characteristics. Make every effort, he says, to build up your spiritual strength. Should he have said (written) instead, "Pray to the Spirit to give you ..."? Some obviously think the apostle was wrong! As we think about praying, by the way, the model prayer taught by Jesus is addressed to God the Father. And as we think about growth in Christ, we might well realize that as we feed on His Word, we just naturally do grow in Him. And as we use our muscles, strength increases.

The bible speaks of several differing baptisms. The particular topic of discussion here has been the baptism commanded by Christ and associated with sinners being brought into Christ's kingdom. Baptism is an immersion. Baptism "into Christ" is the only baptism commanded to be practiced BY Christians. That's why no other baptism could appropriately be called Christian baptism. Here we have referred to baptism into Christ as Christian baptism even though the baptismal candidate is not said to be a Christian until the baptism has taken place. From baptismal waters we are RAISED INTO NEW LIFE. This study has invited readers to look at Bible examples of conversions. It has called attention to what Jesus, and later what His apostles, taught about Christian baptism and being RAISED INTO NEW LIFE.

Bible writers who speak of being raised into new life with Christ apparently do so to make sure their readers will more fully understand what had happened as they were baptized. They clarify what was the significance of the baptism Jesus said was to be performed by those who told others about Him. We study the bible to learn what Jesus wants us to know about baptism, and about the NEW LIFE to follow, and many other matters. It was Jesus who made baptism a necessary step in entering His Way—not just in order to join a particular group of godly people, but in fact to *join with Him*. God's salvation is offered to sinners who will repent and who will be baptized *into Christ.*

God's promise through the apostle Peter is that the Spirit will be given to newborn Christians to help us live for Jesus. But when we decide we need help from the Spirit in order to believe in Jesus and to repent of our sin, we're going beyond what is written by inspiration. Anyone, anywhere, at any time, is free and is capable of believing the gospel and obeying it. The "gift of the Holy Spirit" is given to those who have heard, have believed, and then have obeyed the gospel by repenting and being baptized. Sinners are invited to NOW turn to Christ as Savior and to be baptized into Him, after which they will have received the Spirit to bless and help them walk in Christ's Way. The new birth is of water and spirit—a human spirit which is free to repent or to NOT repent. We are called to love and serve. God's Spirit does not make decisions FOR us. We remain free to live as WE choose, and we face daily decisions either for life or for death.

Based on newfound faith in Jesus and a deliberate turning away from sin, baptism is "for the remission of sins," "to wash away sin," (Acts 22:16) and "to clothe ourselves with (put on) Christ." Christian baptism when performed identifies the newly raised-up individual with the death, burial, resurrection, and life of Jesus Christ. The new birth is of water AND spirit, repentance AND baptism.

***

What is it to die to sin?

Peter uses the word "repent" to call for us to turn away from love of sinning. We turn TO Jesus, to live with Him and for Him in every future day. It's by acts of our will that we are faithful to or unfaithful to Jesus. We are free. God does not force anyone to sin. He does not force us to NOT sin. We make our own decisions. After the Spirit is given, He may help us avoid sin, but we are free moral agents!

***

Did We Learn From Examples?

I hope it became obvious what is common with the inspired reports of conversions. After hearing and believing "the gospel" and TURNING away from sin, they each were baptized and raised into new life. It goes without saying that each conversion came because the sinner did turn away from sin, seeking instead to serve the Savior. Repentance is not mentioned every time, but is sure to have taken place. And repentance and baptism are the elements Jesus (with Peter, Acts 2:38) said make up the new birth (John 3:5). A man of sin was buried (baptized in water) so a man of faith could be raised into new life.

When a Christian sins, the remedy is not trying for another new birth through rebaptism. It's simply repenting and praying. If we repent, God will indeed forgive a Christian's sins. We also see that only those outside of Christ can be or could be baptized "into Christ." Christian baptism following repentance from sin brings outsiders INTO Christian fellowship. Those already IN Christ are forgiven of recognized sin by repenting and praying.

We hope it's clear to every reader that salvation's blessings come only to those believers who both repent AND are baptized. Faith alone, repentance alone, or baptism alone does not save us. A prayer won't do it. The new birth is of water AND the (human) spirit. Having our sins washed away, receiving the "gift of the Holy Spirit," and reconciliation with our God all are ours when our new birth is complete.

Believers come into fellowship with Christ and Christ's people through repentance and baptism. We are outside God's family until we experience new birth. This second birth is completed in the rite of Christian baptism. That's why men of any age are not saved solely by what Jesus did on the cross! Note again what the apostle Paul says on this subject:

> [26]... for in Christ Jesus you are all sons of God, through faith. For *as many of you as were baptized into Christ have put on Christ* (Galatians 3:26,27—ESV, emphasis added).

Inspired teachers always point out and emphasize that it's through faith in Jesus (never by faith alone) that anyone is saved. Paul also places great reliance on our continuing at any cost to tell others that we do now believe in Jesus. To Christians in Rome he wrote:

> [9] ... if you confess with your mouth that Jesus is Lord and believe in your heart that God raised him from the dead, you will be saved. For *with the heart one believes and is justified, and with the mouth one confesses and is saved* (Romans 10:9,10—ESV).

Did the apostle here mean all it takes to become saved is to believe in the resurrection, and all it takes to be justified is to once tell someone we believe in Jesus? We are saved by a faith which leads us to obey! Remember what he wrote in Galatians 3:27 (quoted just above). Paul is saying in Romans chapter ten that those who believe in Jesus are sure to continue to be obedient to Him in all ways. Believing is a way of LIFE. We save ourselves by continuing to believe in Jesus as Lord, and by obeying Him. He's saying we need to continue to believe and at any cost to *continue to say so!*

We now may want to read and re-read the Bible, and continue to think about what IT says in addition on this subject. This will surely interfere with entertainments such as watching TV several hours every day. It will cause us to socialize as a means of sharing the gospel, won't it? That's the NEW LIFE into which we have been invited. We'll no longer want others to serve US, but instead we'll find joy in serving Jesus by serving others.

It's my opinion that every emphasis on what the Spirit may do is de-emphasizing the free will and responsibilities of us humans. It's HUMANS who are exhorted to carry the gospel with us wherever we go in this world. It's HUMANS who are told we should baptize each new believer in Jesus. The message we're to proclaim is about JESUS, not about the Holy Spirit. Why do some want to bring in the Spirit to do what we humans are told to do? Is it to lessen human responsibility and freedom? It's by His own choice that God gave work for HUMANS to do. He could have told the Spirit to do all the things some are claiming He should be doing.

Realize also that it doesn't take a clergyman or clergywoman to perform Christian baptism or to tell others about the risen Lord. *Every Christian is a priest in Christ's church,* fully qualified to speak up for Jesus any time and in any place.

That which accomplishes "new birth of water and spirit" brings the reborn person into the fellowship of God's church. If any reader has not yet been buried with Christ in baptism (immersed in water in Jesus' name), now would be a good time to obey the gospel. Jesus loves us each one. He wants us to enjoy being raised into NEW LIFE with Him and then happily serving Him each day. All Christians should walk in love toward God and toward all men. A pleasant duty.

***

SO WHAT SHOULD WE THINK ABOUT SINNERS BEING RAISED INTO NEW LIFE?

Human birth requires an involvement of both a father and a mother. Jesus said that the "new birth" also required two elements, which were water and spirit. Spiritual change precedes the physical in this spiritual "new birth." Later, the apostle Peter clarifies for our understanding what is the "water and spirit" of new birth. It's a matter of a sinner who now believes in Jesus, in order to receive remission of sins and to receive "the gift of the Holy Spirit," repenting (a spiritual change) and being baptized—immersed into and raised up out of water, as Jesus requires.

Only those who hear the gospel and then choose to live according to the teachings of Jesus can experience the "new birth" of which Jesus spoke in John 3:5. Baptism is a part of this new birth, but it's only the coming out (making viable and visible) of the "new life" which began earlier within the believing sinner's heart (his "spirit"). Life does begin prior to birth. Even so, we speak of human life beginning as the baby is moved outside the home where it was nourished and protected until "outside" life could begin with a good chance of success.

We realize that in one sense life begins at conception rather than at birth. That's why in other Bible verses, most of which we'll not here consider, inspired writers sometimes speak as if the new birth occurred when belief began. But the new birth of water and spirit is not complete without water!

Consider again how new life in Christ begins: New life was conceived when, having heard or read the gospel, the sinner believed the gospel was true. We hope evidence which we've presented and which follows will convince every reader that the actual "new birth" is not completed in faith alone, or in repentance alone, or in simply confessing faith in the Lord Jesus, or even in some special "feeling." None will be in the kingdom of Christ who have not heard the gospel, turned away from sin, and begun walking with Jesus by being buried and RAISED INTO NEW LIFE.

The "new birth" of which Jesus speaks has nothing to do with physical birth or ancestry. Regardless of who our parents were, humans can be born again of water and spirit. But, as in human birth, the new birth of water and spirit is a PROCESS which begins in conception and later culminates in the actual birth experience. The father's role in human birth is called begetting.

We do not usually say a human baby has been born until the birth is complete. The actual birthing is the duty of the mother. Should we think of the new birth of which Jesus spoke as being complete prior to the actual birth? We see the new birth only as we witness the immersion and "resurrection" of one who comes to baptism as a repentant believer in the risen Lord.

Who can doubt that the "new birth" Jesus says is essential for entrance into His kingdom is "of water and spirit?" Immersion alone (that is, water baptism) is not enough. Action by Spirit or spirit is not enough. It's water AND the (human) spirit which bring us into the kingdom and ensure having our sins washed away. Clint Gill points out that water and spirit in this case are "co-ordinate, correlative, and complementary." I think that puts the matter clearly if the words themselves are understood.

Some suppose that baptism is only an introduction into our local church life or to show our family and friends that we have changed. They want to think that we are baptized because we were already saved. They may say or imply that baptism is only a show for our family and friends. Paul says that baptism is for salvation. Baptism is into the death of Christ. It is the point at which the one baptized is seen to die to sin. It's from the waters of baptism that the former sinner is raised up to enjoy new life with Christ. Isn't that what Luke and the apostles in these texts have explained? So then, as the "new birth of water and spirit" which follows believing that Jesus is Lord we are pointed to repentance and baptism into Christ.

ACTS 2:38. OUR LORD's APOSTLE promised his hearers that those who died to sin in repentance and were buried in baptism could then be raised into Spirit-gifted life. They would receive the "gift of God's Holy Spirit." Luke reports that those who "received" (accepted, believed, and were obeying) Peter's MESSAGE were baptized. They were added to the Lord's church, new on that very day. The church was new. These first Christians were new. Now saved. Now sanctified. Set apart for service to Jesus!

Two statements by the apostle Paul, written much later than these by Jesus and Peter, also help us understand the simplicity of "new birth." Paul speaks to our need of "obeying" the gospel. We just above quoted what the apostle wrote to Thessalonian Christians. In Galatians 3:27 Paul makes clear his understanding that it's in Christian baptism that we "put on Christ." Our baptism brings us, he states, "INTO Christ." Is not salvation found only IN Christ? Galatians 3:26,27 should be carefully studied by anyone seeking to be RAISED into NEW LIFE with Christ.

Paul also explains (2 Corinthians 1:22) that a "seal" of our salvation is receiving the Holy Spirit. *"And it is God who establishes us with you in Christ, and has anointed us, and who has also put his seal on us and given us his Spirit in our hearts as a guarantee."* 2 Corinthians 1:21,22—(ESV). We have spoken of this seal as God's life-giving "breath" entering each babe in Christ. Peter had pointed out that those who do repent and who are baptized will *as a result* receive the "gift of the Holy Spirit." Jesus promised HE could be with us throughout our earthly lives. I suggest that the spiritual gift spoken of in Acts 2:38 is the fulfillment of the promise Jesus made of being "with us" to the end of the age.

Neither our baptism nor our resultant receiving of the Spirit took place on the cross. Nor is the gift of the Spirit said to be given prior to, or in any way to cause, the NEW BIRTH of water and spirit. Paul, Jesus, and Peter agree that men of any age must experience a new birth of water and spirit in order to be saved. According to the apostle Peter, men of any age must repent and be baptized in order to enter the kingdom of Christ. It cannot be true then that someone in any condition of life was saved by Jesus in this "church age" except by way of personally experiencing a "new birth," or else as an exception to *the Way Jesus said was the ONLY way to enter.*

WE BAPTIZE BECAUSE Jesus said we should do so. Jesus now has all authority. It's by HIS express desire and in order to obey Him that new believers are buried in water and RAISED INTO NEW LIFE out of the water. Why would any Christian want to NOT obey Jesus as Lord? Why would any Christian doubt that it's AFTER baptism that the new Christian receives the "gift" of the Holy Spirit?

Why was Jesus Himself baptized? Jesus said He was baptized "to fulfill all righteousness." He agreed that his cousin was right that He had no sin and had no need of repentance. Yet He was a Jew. He felt it was necessary and only "right" to do what God had called every Jew to do. So he persuaded John to immerse Him. God sent signs to let both John and Jesus know that the act was correct and that all was well. They saw a descending dove and heard a thundering voice.

We recognize that *any Jew, or any person, who has no sin can be baptized for the same reason as was Jesus.* We who HAVE sinned are not sinless. Every sinner needs to be baptized for the remission of personal sin. How blessed we are to be allowed to repent and be baptized into Christ, then raised into new life with Him! We hope all will see this is true. Haven't we ALL sinned? As was Saul, sinners must "be baptized to wash away ... sin." We are baptized and become disciples of the Christ. What's a disciple?

DISCIPLES ARE LEARNERS. That's what a disciple is. We're students. Jesus asks that we also should "make disciples." We who turn to Jesus for light and life seek to LEARN from Him as well as to teach others what we have learned.

The good example we have from Acts 2 is that disciples then daily sought to learn more about what Jesus did and said. We're told about this in the bible: [42] *"And they devoted themselves to THE APOSTLES' TEACHING and fellowship, to the breaking of bread and the prayers"* (Acts 2:42—ESV, emphasis added).

Just as we can, early disciples could learn from one another. They also could learn by asking questions of the apostles, which we cannot do. But we CAN read the inspired writings which contain apostolic teaching. In our homes and in our church assemblies, should we not diligently pursue *learning of Jesus* through reading (and hearing) the written Word of God? The first Christians also prayed, ate, and shared together.

Through Peter, Jesus has said the first steps to take in entering His Way are for believers to repent and to accept being baptized, then be raised into new life. It's from baptismal waters that repentant, believing sinners are RAISED INTO NEW LIFE! There is no exact English equivalent of the main two Greek words which more than 1,000 years later were transliterated into English by the created English words, "baptize" and "baptism." If they HAD been translated, in most cases the English words chosen would have been "immersed" for the noun, and "immerse" or "bury" for the verb. This is certainly true when the word was used to refer to the actions which through a death, a burial and a resurrection brought and bring outsiders into God's church.

Clint Gill points out that to understand what is taught about Christian immersion in Mark 16:15,16, it is essential to note the sequential order in which Jesus places 1) proclamation, 2) belief, 3) baptism, and then 4) salvation. To say that one who hears the proclamation and believes is saved prior to being immersed is to make Jesus say, "the one 2) believing and 4) being saved shall later be 3) immersed." Is that the same? No. Those who practice "infant baptism" are, in effect, altering His statement to read, "the one 3) being baptized and 4) saved shall later 2) believe." Should we dare to change the promise made by the Lord, and then expect Him to honor what we say but what is not what He did say? No, we must let Jesus speak for Himself. Our responsibility is to listen, believe, and obey Him! Jesus is our Lord! Do we seek to be RAISED INTO NEW LIFE. It's in Jesus Christ life is to be found, and through our obeying the gospel.

Paul says in Romans 6 it's because of our repenting and being baptized into the death of Christ that we now should not sin. IN BAPTISM we were united with the death and resurrection of the Christ. The apostle's appeal is not alone to our faith in Jesus, it's to our realization that because of our new birth of water and spirit we have died to sin. We have been raised up to walk in new life. IN BAPTISM we are united with His death, and with His resurrection. Is baptism just a show? No way! Our repentance and being raised into new life is where the change occurs.

Christian baptism was and is a cleansing, a "washing away" of sin. It seems likely that the earliest Christian believers, because they were familiar with the baptism of converts to Jewry, and because they had become familiar with John's baptism, had little difficulty in understanding the terminology which was used to introduce this new baptism (immersion) "into Christ." God's offer through Peter in Acts 2:38 was conditional: Receive these blessings IF you will change to be ones who from now on will live as Jesus showed us is right. You'll be welcome in the Kingdom of Christ if you now share the goals of God's Son, and if you are willing to live for Him. God didn't offer blessings because some persons had earned or deserved them. Peter explained how *men must change* in order to receive salvation in Jesus. Peter says we save ourselves by repenting and accepting baptism (Acts 2:40,41). The gospel saves those who respond to God's love and who *obey the gospel.*

To repent is to change our preferences and practices. But mere change is not enough. We also must be baptized. In repentance and Christian baptism we die to sin and are buried in order to be raised into new life. Jesus was resurrected. The new birth is of water and spirit. After we turn to Jesus, we accept baptism. Then we continue to obey Jesus, living in and for Him, and walking in our new life. We were RAISED INTO NEW LIFE. Now we live for Jesus. We do see that the new birth is not only of water and equally not only of the spirit. Salvation is by grace through faith. It's God's gift rather than our purchase. Men can't buy or earn cleansing from sin, but we ARE able to begin to do what Jesus wants us to do. Does not Peter say sinners must repent AND be baptized? The change internally and externally is our spiritual rebirth. We who have been buried, then RAISED INTO NEW LIFE with Christ are FREE. We are no longer living under law. Saved by grace, now we live by grace. Christian baptism is a sinner being buried after dying to sin, and then being resurrected into a new life with Jesus!

Christian baptism is to change our status. As the Lord's assembly which we call His "church" began, it was made clear that entrance into this "kingdom" (one not of this world) demanded certain spiritual changes. Old and familiar ways of living were to be discarded. Ones who are satisfied as they are will not see any need to repent and be baptized. Yet, unless we DO repent and are baptized, we die in our sins regardless of all Jesus has done, regardless of how many good deeds we might do on earth.

Today, do not many select their congregation based on what they like rather than what God likes? Their choice is apt to be a church that likes them unchanged, that approves of them as they now are. But Jesus will not accept or save those who love sin and want to continue sinning. He calls for us to NOT remain as we were. He demands that we make needed changes! Those who in humility come to Christ are seeking to BE changed by Him. Jesus is not going to revise the rules for His kingdom to suit us. He offers to help US change to fit in with HIS kingdom the way it was designed from that first Day of Pentecost in Jerusalem in about 30 A.D. Our aim is to live and love as HE did.

We are RAISED INTO NEW LIFE as the climax of being born again of water and spirit. It's by a new birth of water and spirit that any sinner is transformed into a saint. No new births happened on Calvary. Even today sinners must save themselves by obeying the gospel of Christ. Salvation is made possible by what happened at Calvary (Jesus died for us). Individuals "put on Christ" when faith in Him leads them to repent and to be baptized. Cornelius was told that Peter was bringing to him a *message* by which he would be saved. "Would be" is future! And we notice that salvation did not come through baptism in or by the Spirit! It never does.

Obeying the gospel saves when we die to sin and are RAISED INTO NEW LIFE. We turned away from sin. We turned to Jesus. We learned that Jesus loves us and wants us to enjoy ETERNAL life. He wants us to enjoy this life on earth also. Raised into NEW LIFE. We no longer enjoy living selfishly. He calls us to deny self, take up a symbol of DEATH and walk in life as a servant, thinking more of others than of self. This way leads to real joy.

Christian baptism is new and different. John the Baptist, and John's disciples and disciples of Jesus had also baptized people "for the remission of sins." The baptism by John, as is Christian baptism, was by command of God. John was called to prepare the way for the coming kingdom and to baptize all repentant Jews. But the baptism which Jesus Christ commands for repentant sinners then and now, is because the kingdom HAS BEGUN. We hope each who experienced the baptism of John also felt cleansed from sin. But when the church began, there was an additional promise connected with this *new* baptism. Peter now promises to those who because of faith in JESUS do repent and are baptized both remission of sins AND "the gift of the Holy Spirit." John's baptism conveyed no such gift as becoming indwelt by God! Should those who now receive Baptist baptism seek to complete the new birth of water and spirit?

God and Jesus choose to dwell within those who have chosen to obey the gospel. Saved Christians are now temples where GOD lives. Note that this "gift of the Holy Spirit" for all who do repent and accept baptism into Christ is not at all the special spiritual powers which were transmitted by the laying on of hands by Christ's apostles. This gift of the Spirit conveys to us no powers, just the assurance that wherever we go God is in us and with us. That God now dwells in humans is miraculous, but it doesn't empower us who have been baptized to perform any miracles at all.

In early days of the church, miracles were frequent rather than rare. Many were being healed. Prophets were speaking directly from God to His people. Some were enabled to speak languages they had never learned. Others understood what was said in the language unknown by the speaker. Many strange things are prophesied by the writer of the last words in the gospel according to Mark:

> [15] And he said to them, "Go into all the world and proclaim the gospel to the whole creation. Whoever believes and is baptized will be saved, but whoever does not believe will be condemned. And these signs will accompany those who believe: in my name they will cast out demons; they will speak in new tongues; they will pick up serpents with their hands; and if they drink any deadly poison, it will not hurt them; they will lay their hands on the sick, and they will recover" (Mark 16:15-18—ESV, emphasis added).

All these promised miracles were seen in that generation They were done by persons who had received from the apostles power to perform "special" spiritual things. In some "missionary" locations particularly, some of these signs are still being seen, I'm told. Handling poisonous snakes and drinking poisons are not recommended spiritual exercises for Christians today. Cheerful service by all of us is possible and expected.

Christian baptism is not "work" in any sense. Let's realize that being raised into new life is not something done BY the one being baptized. It's done TO that person. A sinner can work all he (or she) wants to and still could not succeed in burying himself and raising himself out of a "watery grave." The sinner is placed UNDER the water by the hands of another person, and then is immediately lifted up OUT OF the water, still by the hands of another person. The sinner does no work. The raising into new life is done by someone other than the sinner who is being saved.

Being baptized is just submitting to an act that JESUS said was to be performed upon anyone as soon as the person came to believe in the risen Lord and wanted to make Jesus his Lord. The next time you hear someone refer to being baptized as a work, you will do well to point out to the speaker that they're misunderstanding what is happening when a person is baptized. The one receiving baptism is doing NO work at all. The immersing is not done by, but is done TO the one being baptized. We do well to remember that it was JESUS who commanded baptism for new converts, which is why apostles baptized. Do we also see that faith and repentance always preceded the baptisms? And we'll realize that it was AFTER conversion that the Spirit is given! Apostles knew every sinner needed a new birth of water and spirit. The baptizing was ordered by JESUS, not by any man. Who will say Jesus was wrong? Many do. They would do well to not suppose Jesus didn't know what He was talking about. They're brave to dare to criticize Jesus and think they know more than He.

Being raised into new life is serious business. Christian baptism is not to be performed unthinkingly or as if it were unimportant. Those who want to become Christians do so by repenting and being baptized. Jesus is our Lord. We baptize in obedience to our Master. Quickly. Right away. Those who respect Jesus will not think or speak lightly of what HE commands. The invitation to repent and be baptized is open to every person. There's no limit on who can repent and be baptized. The only limit is that one who does NOT die to sin cannot be raised into new life.

No committee or human power is entitled to decide who deserves baptism. No church body has the right to decide whether or not baptism can be performed upon any seeker. Jesus has commanded that immersion SHALL be done. He makes no provision for us deciding whether or not it's appropriate or proper. Our obedience of performing baptisms is done by order of our Lord. Why would anyone want to baptize except that Jesus said we should do so? Immersing which is not done by His authority and in HIS name is not Christian baptism. We don't speak of special ritualistic speech which makes the act "kosher." We speak of the authority by which the deed is done. *We baptize to please God rather than men.*

Christian baptism is by free choice. Of course we bury and raise into new life only those who WANT to be baptized! Did we even need to mention the fact? But how does a person know they should be baptized? Our sharing the gospel should without fail include our telling of the need those outside of Christ have to repent and BE baptized. That's how they will know they should be baptized. We TELL them. If they read the bible they will learn from it about baptism. So what kind of a disciple of Christ is it who urges sinners to come to Christ by performing something OTHER than being baptized? Many do have other invitations. Some suggest reciting a "sinner's prayer," saying this will bring the sinner "into Christ." No, it won't. Paul and Jesus and Peter point to the right Way. The Way into Christ's kingdom is by hearing and believing the gospel, then repenting and being baptized. That's how it was done on the birthday of the church. God hasn't changed His mind about how sinners become saints. The JESUS Way remains the one Way that washes sin away.

ACTS 2:38; The apostle Peter promises two wonderful results from baptism of penitent believers in Jesus. Neither is sure to be "felt" by the one being baptized. First, God wipes the slate clean in heaven where books are kept which record our deeds. Sin is washed away. It is no longer counted against us. On the record, it's as if we were newly born, as in fact we are. RAISED INTO NEW LIFE! This result of baptism is based entirely upon our faith in the risen Lord. We have no reason to trust in baptism itself or even water of softest texture to wash away sin. We need not trust the baptizer. It's JESUS we trust. It's Jesus who points out that the new birth is of water and spirit, and who then through Peter calls for us to both repent AND be baptized in order to be saved.

When we do so, He keeps His promise. He cleanses us from our sin. Secondly, He gifts us with His Spirit. Those who repent and are baptized are THEN given the Spirit. After we are baptized, the closer we walk with Jesus the more we are apt to feel His presence and sense Him "within" us. Jesus is our Lord. Jesus is our Savior. Jesus is our friend. Jesus is the one who commanded that each new believer is to be baptized. Some presume they have some right to vote on whether or not to obey the

Lord's command. Will their ignorance be excused? Why would it?

Christian baptism is immersion in water, then being raised into new life! Jesus commanded that humans are to perform this act. It is not performed by Jesus or by His Holy Spirit. Neither faith nor confession of faith can take the place of repentance and baptism (new birth of water and spirit "into Christ"). Only we who do believe in Jesus will obey Him. Of course we also tell others of our faith. How could we not do so? The climax of the new birth is when our "old man of sin" is buried and then we are raised up from baptismal water to walk in a life of service and love for all God's people.

Note that we cannot hate other people and also love the God who LOVES them. The more we love others, the more we will be like Jesus who loves so much that He wants EVERYONE to be saved. Life in the time in which Christ's apostles lived was in some ways similar to today. Enemies of the Christ were powerful and pervasive. They controlled the government, therefore could make and enforce whatever laws they wished. Christians were persecuted. Christians were martyred. Christians were faithful. So should we be at all times and in all ways.

Christians then were convinced that what Jesus offers is far better than was elsewhere available. This is still true. They chose to live for Jesus despite incredible odds. It was in future days they expected glory and peace. It's still that way! Many Christians today face torment and torture at the hands of enemies of Jesus Christ. He is worth it. Be reminded that no one is asked to believe in baptism. *We accept baptism because of faith in JESUS.* He commanded it. His apostles practiced it because the Lord said to practice it. Their motive is our motive as well. We want to please our Lord.

WHAT FOLLOWS NEW BIRTH INTO CHRIST?

We have been RAISED INTO NEW LIFE. Of course now we will live FOR HIM. We need to regulate our beliefs and our practice by what God teaches. Is it not so? Our words should be carefully chosen to reveal God's truth and never to conceal it. We ask ourselves, "WERE we buried with Christ? ARE we now walking in new life?" If we experienced the new birth Jesus speaks of in John 3:5, we HAVE been buried and resurrected with Christ. We repented. We accepted baptism into Christ. We now ARE reborn. Jesus now lives within us! We have been RAISED INTO NEW LIFE with Christ.

Yet we face persecution and death if we confess that we do believe Jesus is Lord. We need to be faithful unto death, not expecting only peace and prosperity if we are followers of one who earned our redemption by DYING for us. We follow One who endured greatly "for the glory that was set before Him." We also are called to serve and wait for glory which will last forever.

In this generation, many are faced with the same dilemma presented long ago to Roman soldiers. Swear allegiance to the god who is your political ruler or die. Name Caesar as your lord. Those then who knew Jesus was Lord had no choice. We who know Jesus is Lord also have no choice. God is. Jesus is. Jesus has conquered death and offers us eternal life. Of course we will confess that we do believe Jesus is Lord. Won't we?

All are saved who hear the gospel and obey its call for sinners to turn away from sin in order to serve Jesus instead, and to be baptized to seal their calling. Age is no barrier. Social status means nothing in seeking membership in God's kingdom. Both men and women are welcome, as are all children old enough to make sensible decisions concerning their future. No one is too poor to be accepted. No one is so rich that his riches will cause him to be rejected so long as the person is not in love with things of this world. What Paul is saying is that in Christ's church we should find no barriers to fellowship with every other member. We should love every saved Christian.

CONFESSION OF FAITH is telling something about a Savior rather than about sins of the believer. Some brag about how bad they were until they turned to Christ. We do well to put such evil deeds behind us and not keep reminding ourselves of them.

***

All kinds of mischief can come in the wake of believing that in some way the Spirit of God is involved in the new birth of water and spirit. A 2009 graduate of a Christian-worker training college of my acquaintance [I received a BA(Ministerial) degree there in 1955] stated in my hearing that he knew of a Muslim who was converted to Christ by a dream rather than by the gospel. The man is said to have felt that the Holy Spirit had inspired the dream so the man wanted to be baptized, perhaps to keep in touch with the spirit of which he had dreamed. But there are many spirits in the world. There were in Jesus' time. There ARE in our time. These spirits are especially active in less-educated areas, poorer areas, and where witch-doctors or Muslim clerics have influence. Or where religious teachers of many non-Christian persuasions practice witchcraft by any name.

Is it only ignorance which opens people to the influence of evil spirits which often masquerade as good ones? No, but that helps. However some wealthy and well-educated people, even ones who attend and hold membership in churches, are influenced by spirits other than the Holy Spirit of God. For example, those who cast horoscopes, who tell fortunes, who feel they should be influenced by particular placement of stars.

What I understand the young Bible teacher to be saying is that we need to depend on action of the Spirit today when we preach about Jesus. Hearing the gospel is not enough, he thinks, the Spirit determines who will respond to Christ's gospel. This book presents the gospel of CHRIST. It does not depend on spirits. The gospel interacts with human spirits to result in some sinners choosing to repent of sin. The simple story of God who came to earth and was put to death in thanks by unappreciative men is the gospel. Jesus offers salvation to every man. His offer is that any sinner who seeks to be joined to Him must accept new birth of water and spirit.

The new birth is NOT something mystic and hidden. It happens out of sight, yes. It's not mysterious. People hear about a God of love and His unique Son who loved so much that He paid for sinners the price of sin. Having heard, some turn to Jesus and turn away from sinful thoughts and deeds. We call this repenting. The one who now is a repentant believer in Jesus as Lord and Savior is then buried in water and raised out of the water to walk in NEW LIFE with Jesus as Lord. We can't see repentance. We can't see faith. It happens within a person. If it's real, it leads to new life!

What's wrong with a salvation based on feelings rather than facts? Feelings may change. Facts remain true. How about someone who rejects the gospel but fears a dream, can that person be baptized and saved by his fear? Not unless the fear causes the person to HEAR the gospel, believe it, and obey it! The motive which is Biblical is NOT fear. Any Christian who seeks to save the lost better go to them with the GOSPEL rather than with a suggestion they seek a dream or vision in order to think they're saved by the "experience."

Much that happens during conversion into Jesus is unseen, yet it happens just the same. One person hears of and believes in a risen Lord. Realizing his sin, he repents of sin. Turning away from sin, the person can find LIFE and peace and love in God's unique Son. At God's direction and in the name of Jesus, a person buries another person, a repentant, believing sinner, in water and quickly raises that person back out of the water, *raised into new life* with Jesus as companion and guide. God looks on with pleasure and approval. Sin is washed away. Jesus adds a name to the Lamb's Book of Life.

A simple transaction. From death to life. The Lord Jesus does it. The Spirit of God and Jesus is sent to help a new Christian learn and live for Jesus. And the "babe in Christ" has a life of service to live with joy and Spirit-help in overcoming any problem. God is good.

***

Victor Knowles is founder and director of POEM (Peace on Earth Ministries), Joplin, MO. Please notice what he has written about baptism into Christ and the NEW LIFE which follows new birth.

BAPTISM OF EACH REPENTANT BELIEVER IS BEING RAISED INTO NEW LIFE

by VICTOR KNOWLES

United States Senator Sam Houston was baptized November 19, 1854 in Little Rocky Creek near Independence, Texas. It is said that the two people who had the most influence on leading Houston from a life of sin to Christ were his wife Margaret and Baines Johnson (great-grandfather of President Lyndon Baines Johnson). It is said that when Houston arose from the waters of baptism he exclaimed, "God have mercy on the fish!"

Baptism is mentioned more than 120 times in the Bible. The noun "baptism" and the verb "baptize" are anglicized Greek words that mean "to dip, plunge, or immerse." "The simple act of a new believer being immersed into Christ is a divine drama that illustrates beautifully the washing away of sins by the blood of Jesus and the rising to walk in a new life by faith in the resurrected Christ" (Bob Russell, THE LOOKOUT, January 20, 2002). Baptism was the first public act of Jesus' ministry. He walked about 70 miles to be immersed in the Jordan River by his cousin, John the Baptist (Matthew 3:13-17). After his baptism, the heavens were opened, the Holy Spirit descended in the form of a dove, and God's voice was heard: "this is My beloved Son, in whom I am well pleased" (Matthew 3:17, New King James Version). ...

Baptism was part of the last command given by Jesus on earth. Jesus said, "All authority In heaven and on earth has been given to me. Therefore go and make disciples of all nations, baptizing them in the name of the Father and of the Son and of the Holy Spirit" (Matthew 28:18,19). Baptism is the only command in the Bible given in the name of the Godhead.

Baptism in the New Testament

Each of the nine accounts of conversion in the book of Acts culminates in Christian baptism. Believers repented of their sins, confessed Christ, and were baptized. They did not balk at baptism. They did not belittle baptism. They did not bide their time. From the Day of Pentecost onward, baptism was always an immediate faith response to the gospel of grace heard and believed.

In his book Baptism Today and Tomorrow (St. Martin's Press, 1966), G. R. Beasley-Murray finds five attendant blessings to baptism in the New Testament:

1. Forgiveness of sins (Acts 2:38; 22:16),
2. Union with Christ (Galatians 3:26,27; Colossians 2:12; Romans 6:1-11),
3. Possession of the Holy Spirit (Acts 2:38; Titus 3:5),
4. Membership in the church (1 Corinthians 12:13),
5. Inheritance of the kingdom of God (John 3:5).

Beasley-Murray concludes, "In the light of these statements I am compelled to conclude that the understanding of baptism as 'a beautiful and expressive symbol,' and nothing more, is irreconcilable with the New Testament."

The apostle Paul wrote often about baptism in his epistles. Baptism is the threshold of entrance into Christ, his atoning death, and his glorious church. Paul states that we are "baptized into Christ" (Galatians 3:27), "baptized into his death" (Romans 6:3), and "baptized into one body" (1 Corinthians 12:13). The footnotes of several Bible translations indicate that the Great Commission as recorded in Matthew may also read "baptizing them into the name of the Father and of the Son and of the Holy Spirit" (Matthew 28:19). Baptism, then, brings a convert into a new relationship "where God becomes his heavenly Father, God's Son becomes his personal Savior, and God's Spirit becomes his indwelling strength" (The Beauty of Baptism, by Alger Fitch, 2003).

Baptism and the Cross

Recently Timothy George, executive editor of Christianity Today, answered a question from a reader in his column "Good Question." The question was, "What is the role of baptism in faith and salvation?" George responded, in part, "Baptism must take place in the context of faith, and it must connect to the central events of the gospel—Jesus' cross and resurrection" (CT, July 2003). This is precisely the point the apostle Paul makes in Romans 6:1-4, where he writes, "What shall we say, then? Shall we go on sinning so that grace may increase? By no means! We died to sin; how can we live in it any longer? Or don't you know that all of us who were baptized into Christ Jesus were baptized into his death? We were therefore buried with him through baptism into death that, just as Christ was raised from the dead through the glory of the Father, we too may live a new life."

Baptism certainly connects to the central events of the gospel! We are "baptized into Christ Jesus." We are "baptized into his death." We are "buried with him through baptism into death." We are raised "just as Christ was raised from the dead." It's all there in baptism—death, burial, and resurrection. The passage in Romans is more clearly understood when placed alongside what Paul wrote to the Corinthians when he defined the gospel. He said, "that Christ died for our sins according to the Scriptures, that he was buried, that he was raised on the third day according to the Scriptures" (1 Corinthians 15:3,4). The gospel is the death, burial, and resurrection of Christ—as it is portrayed in Scripture. The response to the gospel is our death, burial, and resurrection—as it is portrayed in Christian baptism.

Baptism is more than a commemoration of what has already happened in the sinner. It is a dynamic action, an actual participation, a life-changing event. We are buried with Christ. We are baptized into his death. There we die with Christ. We are raised with Christ, just as he was raised. The saving power in this act is linked to the resurrection of Christ (1 Peter 3:21). All this is indeed an act of faith that God is graciously doing something special at this time. "Having been buried with him in baptism and raised with him through your faith in the power of God, who raised him from the dead" (Colossians 2:12).

Martin Luther said, "Your baptism is nothing less than grace clutching you by the throat: a grace-full throttling, by which your sin is submerged in order that ye may remain under grace. Come thus to thy baptism. Give thyself up to be drowned in baptism and killed by the mercy of thy dear God, saying: 'Drown me and throttle me, dear Lord, for henceforth I will gladly die to sin with thy Son'" (as quoted in Down in the River to Pray, John Mark Hicks and Greg Taylor, Leafwood Publishers, 2003). The death to sin, the burial of a dead sinner, and the resurrection of a new person all occur in baptism.

Baptism has been likened to a tomb. Alger Fitch says baptism is a tomb in that “the person buried in the tomb of water is to have died to self. Eyes, ears, lips are under the wave. Sex organs, hands, feet, and mind are now ready to rise into a life over which Jesus is to have control. The total surrender of a total person to the total will of God is what baptism confesses.” Baptism can also be likened to a womb where one is born again of the water and of the spirit (John 3:5; 1 Corinthians 12:12,13).

Baptism and the New Life

New life, free from the dominion of sin, is the result of our baptism into the death of Christ. Norma McCorvey (of “Roe vs. Wade” notoriety) was baptized on August 8, 1995. The same day was her last day of employment at a Dallas abortion clinic. She testified, “I’ll serve the Lord and help women save their babies for the rest of my life.” Former NFL great and TV broadcaster Pat Summerall, who nearly ruined his life with alcohol, was recently baptized. He said, “I went down into the water, and when I came up it was like a 40-pound weight had been lifted from me. I have a happier life, a healthy life, and a more positive feeling about life than ever before."

Here’s the bottom line on baptism: So what do we do? Keep on sinning so God can keep on forgiving? I should hope not! If we’ve left the country where sin is sovereign, how can we still live in our old house there? Or didn’t you realize we packed up and left there for good? That is what happened in baptism. When we went under the water, we left the old country of sin behind; when we came up out of the water, we entered into the new country of grace—a new life in a new land! That’s what baptism into the life of Jesus means? (Romans 6:1-3 The Message).

***

CONCERNING THE WORD OF GOD

by CECIL MAY JR.
of Faulkner University in Alabama.

The word of God is the means by which God both communicates and acts (Genesis 1&2). "For he spoke, and it came to be; he commanded, and it stood firm" (Psalm 33:9). When Jesus is accused of "making himself equal with God" (John 5:18), he responds not by denying the claim but by demonstrating that the Father has given him two things that only God can do: give life, and execute judgment (John 5:21-23). Jesus accomplishes both by the power of his word. For him, as well as for the Father, he acts by speaking. He causes things to be by telling them to be.

Jesus declares, "Truly, truly, I say to you, an hour is coming, and is now here, when the dead will hear the voice of the Son of God, and those who hear will live" (John 5:25). He is speaking of the power of his word, the power of the gospel, to transform the spiritually dead, and to give them spiritual life. He backs that up by adding, "Do not marvel at this, for an hour is coming when all who are in the tombs will hear his voice and come out, those who have done good to the resurrection of life, and those who have done evil to the resurrection of judgment" (5:28,29).

We know the power of his word to raise the dead. His command, "Lazarus, come out," put life back into a decaying corpse and brought Lazarus alive from a tomb. As Marshall Keeble said, "If Jesus had not called Lazarus by name, every body in that cemetery would have come out of their tomb." The word of that same Jesus, who is God, will at the last day, indeed, raise every person who has ever died out of whatever grave or state they may be in, to a renewal of conscious existence. A reformed, converted alcoholic was taunted by old drinking friends, "Do you really believe your Jesus turned plain water into good wine at Cana in Galilee?" "I believe he did," the man said, "because the Bible says so. Besides, I saw him turn beer, wine and whiskey into food, furniture and clothes at my house." That is the power of the gospel to change lives today.

 The word of God, scripture, is the seed from which we are born again (1 Peter 1:23). It is the light by which we are directed (Psalm 119:105), the food on which we feed (Hebrews 5:13,14), the foundation on which we are built (Ephesians 2:20). It builds us up (Acts 20:32). It is the truth by which we are sanctified (John 17:17). It is the word which is able to save our souls (James 1:21). It is the standard by which one day the whole world will be judged (John 12:48). Never deprecate the word of God. God acts through his word. Gladly receive it to be saved and transformed by it.—Cecil May Jr., Faulkner University. These remarks were published in *PREACHER TALK,* Vol.25, No.1, July, 2010.

***

In THE LOOKOUT magazine for 7/25/10 is a brief essay. It's by David Faust, who writes regularly for THE LOOKOUT. I wish every person in the world could read and believe what David has written concerning us who have been raised into new life.

CAN WE MEASURE GOD'S LOVE?

By David Faust, Cincinnati Bible Seminary

In America we resist the metric system, but we have a meter for everything: odometers, thermometers, barometers, speedometers. We measure our trips in miles and hours, our height in feet and inches, our weight in pounds (and sighs). At school we measure grades; at work we measure productivity; at church we measure attendance and offerings. We keep track of sales goals and voter polls, salaries and calories, horsepower and miles per hour. We measure blue jeans and TV screens, package weights and interest rates, fat grams and Virginia hams. We attempt to measure maturity by adding up a person's birthdays. A rule of thumb in business declares, "If it can't be measured, it doesn't matter."

What about God's love? Can it be measured? In Ephesians 3:18, the apostle Paul prays that God's people "may have power, together with all the saints, to grasp how wide and long and high and deep is the love of Christ." How wide is God's love? Broad enough to encompass every era in human history. Expansive enough to override political barriers. Spacious enough to embrace every age, language, and ethnic group on earth. Ample enough to forgive sin without cheapening justice. Wide enough to take a diverse array of men, women, boys, and girls who have next to nothing in common and make them one in Christ.

How long is God's love? So long it stretches into eternity. So long it reaches back to Adam and forward to the final judgment—back to the days of our ancestors and forward to the days of our great-grandchildren—back to Christ's death and forward to his return. How high is it? Taller than a redwood tree, loftier than a mountain peak, elevated above the moon and sun. God's love "reaches to the heavens" and his "faithfulness to the skies" (Psalm 36:5). It soars beyond the farthest galaxy, beyond the reach of our strongest telescope, beyond what mortal eyes can see. How deep is it? According to geology.com, the North Pacific's Mariana Trench contains the deepest point in the earth's oceans, some 35,840 feet below sea level. If Mount Everest were placed at this location it would be covered by a mile of water. Yet, God's cavernous love is so vast that he will "hurl all our iniquities into the depths of the sea" (Micah 7:19).

"God loves you." Who can measure the impact of those simple words? God not only "so loved the world," he so loves you. You are not a mistake or a miscalculation. You are not an afterthought, an oversight, or an underdog. You are not a nobody on your way to nowhere. You don't have to be a lone wolf or a lost sheep. In Christ you are not forgotten or forsaken, but forgiven. You are not worthless, but worthwhile. Life is not pointless, but purposeful. The one who created the universe places infinite value on you. He considers you a treasure worthy of his personal attention and sacrifice.

No mind can comprehend it, no scale can measure it, and no price tag can determine its value, but it's true. "Neither death nor life, neither angels nor demons, neither the present nor the future, nor any powers, neither height nor depth, nor anything else in all creation, will be able to separate us from the love of God that is in Christ Jesus our Lord" (Romans 8:38,39).

***

A BIBLE is the best guidebook anyone can have for living and enjoying the NEW LIFE into which we are raised with Christ. But we don't normally read a Bible as if it were a newspaper or a novel or an essay. In a companion book we offer suggestions on how best to learn from and live as ones who act based on the Word of God. PROPER Bible Understanding is possible! We joyfully enter NEW LIFE with Christ as babes in Christ. We are expected to GROW in grace and knowledge of both God and man. Children deserve nurture and love from more mature people. Every Christian is daily at risk, for Satan seeks us as prey night and day. Bible study helps us grow. Serving others in Christ's name helps us grow. Our aim as ones who are RISEN INTO NEW LIFE should be to grow each day to be more like JESUS in thoughts and deeds.

***

Do we disrespect the Father? *Are we ignoring the Spirit?* Some suggest that believing Jesus saves through new birth of water and the human spirit implies that God the Father and His Holy Spirit are being left out of the picture by mistake. They may not realize that conversion of sinner to saint depends on functions long ago put in place.

Peter was not saying that human merit saved those who repented and were baptized. He was not slighting the part God played in making salvation available! He was only pointing out that NOW it was the sinner who needed to do something to be saved! The Father had already acted. The price had been paid.

Just as gravity was put in place once for all, so is salvation's price already paid. And the written Word which convicts the world of sin is already in place. It does not have to be redone each time a sinner seeks salvation.

Many today have added human traditions to the Way and are now teaching that you must be baptized, and then must follow their human laws in order to remain in Christ. Galatians deals with works of the Mosaic Law. Today, Paul would have needed to fight against human laws no less than laws based on keeping the Old Testament law code.

***

In Romans 6:12-19 the apostle Paul urges:

> [12] Let not sin therefore reign in your mortal bodies, to make you obey their passions. Do not present your members to sin as instruments for unrighteousness, but present yourselves to God as those who have been brought from death to life, and your members to God as instruments for righteousness. For sin will have no dominion over you, since you are not under law but under grace.
>
> [15] What then? Are we to sin because we are not under law but under grace? By no means! Do you not know that if you present yourselves to anyone as obedient slaves, you are slaves of the one whom you obey, either of sin, which leads to death, or of obedience, which leads to righteousness? But thanks be to God, that you who were once slaves of sin have become obedient from the heart to the standard of teaching to which you were committed, and, having been set free

 from sin, have become slaves of righteousness. I am speaking in human terms, because of your natural limitations. For just as you once presented your members as slaves to impurity and to lawlessness leading to more lawlessness, so now present your members as slaves to righteousness leading to sanctification.

*** 30 ***

INDEX AND LIST OF SCRIPTURES USED IN THIS STUDY

FOREWORD (page 1). People live on the earth. A good force created the earth and each of us. The good force is God. People can be good or we can be bad. Doing bad things is sin. God invites all to join Him in being good and rejecting bad. People must act to reject badness. God has spoken to tell us how we can choose good over evil. We live and later will die. Two destinations lie ahead. Heaven is for those who serve God on earth. Hell is for others who chose to be bad. People are free to choose. God gave the Bible to guide us to Him.

The Bible tells how we can please God. This book explains God's call to goodness. We who do bad things are sinners. If we want to please God we will turn away from all bad things. We will choose to live as God's unique Son lived while on earth.

PREFACE. (page 3) Three Bible passages in particular speak to the need of bad people changing. Witness 1, Witness 2, and Witness 3. We explain our plan for study of "new birth" into Christ. Changing from bad to good involves a complete change of ownership. To follow Jesus means making HIM our Lord. He calls for us to experience a new birth of water and spirit if we want to be His followers. In any birth, Birth follows conception. Of course it's the same sequence in the new birth into Christ.

INTRODUCTION (page 7) tells of John the Baptist. God sent a prophet to prepare the way for Jesus to teach and then to open the way for bad people to change and become good people. John baptized Jews with "Baptist baptism" and won many converts to repentance and baptism for remission of sins. One who came to

John was Jesus. Jesus was baptized. His baptism was unique. This is followed by some background facts.

What did Jesus say about new birth? (page 11) It's Jesus & Nicodemus who first discuss a new birth of water and spirit. We note His statement. We speak to the new birth of water and to baptism in His Spirit by Jesus. Then we speak about what JESUS told His apostles to do to bring others into God's family. Mark words the commission differently.

Early Disciples Were Born Again. (page 16) The apostles obeyed Jesus. They proclaimed gospel truth. They baptized those who believed. (page 17) The Gospel message saves. The new (Christian) baptism is not John's baptism. And God's GIFT was given then and promised also for all who later obeyed the gospel. Samaritans then were saved. (page 18) We learn something when two SIMONS met. (page 19) Then Philip met an Ethiopian and both were glad. (page 21) Later, Paul was reborn.(page 23) And Cornelius was visited with surprising results. (page 24) Speaking of surprises, A jailer was jolted, then baptized! (page 29) These are the reported conversions. What did we learn?

Apostles speak so we can understand conversion into Christ. (pages 30-52) What shall we think? If it's true, we should admit we believe. We must choose: Repent or perish! We are all baptized INTO Jesus as we're born again of water and spirit. Paul met controversy in Galatian churches when enemies came with a different gospel (pages 37-40). The word translated as "spirit" means spirit OR breath. God breathes to start each new life when sinners are saved (page 41). So why do we baptize? (pages 48,65) And why do we assemble? (page 50) The NEW Birth converts sinners into saints in the making. Then as ONE body we grow. And we should keep learning.

Conclusions are clear. (pages 53-76) Seed which produces new life is the gospel. (page 53). This is what Paul taught that some didn't like. Conception's "Seed," is God's WORD. (page 53) * Are Only Some Elected To Salvation?, (page 54) * When is God's Spirit given? (page 55) * People baptize people. (page 56) * ALL sinners can be saved. (page 54). When is the Spirit given? (page 55). Jesus calls for proclaimers to baptize! (page 56). The apostle says baptism is "putting on Christ." (page 64). Disciples are learners (page 66). Baptism into Christ cleanses from sin (page 64-67) It's new and different from any other baptism. (page 69) Work it is NOT. (page 70) It IS serious business. (page 71) Baptism must be by free choice. (page 72) Some wonder, "When are we saved?" (pages 72,73). Baptism into Christ is always immersion in water of a repentant believer, who is THEN raised into new life. (page 73)

A Warning. Some Seek To Bypass NEW BIRTH. (page 74) * Victor Knowles Speaks to the Question. (page 77) * Cecil May Jr. ON GOD'S WORD. (page 81) * David Faust Offers Hope (page 83).

***

SCRIPTURES:

9658776R0005

Made in the USA
Charleston, SC
30 September 2011